Jackie Robinson

with profiles of
Satchel Paige
and Branch Rickey

World Book, Inc.
a Scott Fetzer company
Chicago

BIOGRAPHICAL CONNECTIONS

Writer: Timothy D. Frystak.

World Book, Inc.
233 N. Michigan Ave.
Chicago, IL 60601

For information about other World Book publications, visit our Web site at **www.worldbook.com** or call **1-800-WORLDBK (967-5325)**. For information about sales to schools and libraries, call **1-800-975-3250 (United States)**, or **1-800-837-5365 (Canada)**.

Library of Congress Cataloging-in-Publication Data

Frystak, Timothy D.
  Jackie Robinson: with profiles of Satchel Paige and Branch Rickey / [writer, Timothy D. Frystak].
    p. cm. -- (Biographical connections)
  Summary: "A biography of Jackie Robinson, with profiles of two prominent individuals, who are associated through the influences they had on one another, the successes they achieved, or the goals they worked toward. Includes recommended readings and web sites"--Provided by publisher.
  Includes bibliographical references and index.
  ISBN-13: 978-0-7166-1828-7
  ISBN-10: 0-7166-1828-1
  1. Robinson, Jackie, 1919-1972--Juvenile literature. 2. Baseball players--United States--Biography--Juvenile literature. 3. Discrimination in sports--United States--History. 4. Baseball--United States--History. 5. Paige, Satchel, 1906-1982--Juvenile literature. 6. Rickey, Branch, 1881-1965--Juvenile literature. I. World Book, Inc. II. Title. III. Series.
  GV865.R6F79 2007
  796.357092--dc22
  [B]
                                        2006017515

Printed in the United States of America
1 2 3 4 5 10 09 08 07 06

Contents

Acknowledgments

The publisher gratefully acknowledges the following sources for the photographs in this volume.

Cover	AP/Wide World
	© National Baseball Hall of Fame
	AP/Wide World
7	©National Baseball Hall of Fame
15	© George Strock, Time Life Pictures/Getty Images
17	AP/Wide World
21	© George Silk, Time Life Pictures/Getty Images
24	© Louis Requena, MLB Photos Getty Images
27-34	AP/Wide World
36	© National Baseball Hall of Fame
37	AP/Wide World
42	© National Baseball Hall of Fame
45	© National Baseball Hall of Fame/Getty Images
47	© National Baseball Hall of Fame
51-56	AP/Wide World
59	© National Baseball Hall of Fame/Getty Images
60	AP/Wide World
64	© Time Life Pictures/Getty Images
65	© Corbis/Bettmann
67-76	AP/Wide World
79	© National Baseball Hall of Fame
82-89	AP/Wide World
95	© National Baseball Hall of Fame/Getty Images
99	© George Silk, Time Life Pictures/Getty Images
102	© National Baseball Hall of Fame
106	© George Silk, Time Life Pictures/Getty Images

Preface

Biographical Connections takes a contextual approach in presenting the lives of important people. In each volume, there is a biography of a central figure. This biography is preceded and followed by profiles of other individuals whose lifework connects in some way to that of the central figure. The three subjects are associated through the influences they had on one another, the successes they achieved, or the goals they worked toward. The series includes men and women from around the world and throughout history in a variety of fields.

Baseball is a sport so popular in the United States that it is often called the "national pastime." Many Little Leaguers have imagined themselves rounding the bases in the big leagues after swatting a game-winning homer—or perhaps pitching a no-hitter or the winning game in the World Series.

The three people featured in this volume all shared the dream of playing in the big leagues. For Leroy "Satchel" Paige and Jackie Robinson, a dream is all it seemed it would remain—until a historic decision was made by Branch Rickey to open the major leagues to all men equally, regardless of race.

In the first part of the 1900's—until 1947—African Americans were not allowed to play major league baseball alongside white ballplayers. For immensely talented black athletes, such as Paige and Robinson, that left no chance of fulfilling the dream. For decades, when African American players took to the field, it was always in the Negro leagues.

Paige was one of the greatest pitchers in his day. He was even able to strike out many big leaguers in exhibition games. There was no denying that the major leagues could use Satchel Paige. However, because he was black, the door to the majors was closed to him.

The door began to open in 1947 when Rickey, a white man who was the general manager of a team called the Brooklyn Dodgers, signed Robinson to a major league contract. Rickey knew it was wrong not to allow these talented men the opportunity to play major league baseball, but many people disagreed with him. Rickey was committed to gaining equality for black players in the major leagues, and he developed and implemented a plan for integrating the game. It took a special player to help implement this change—a player who was not only talented, but who also had determination, courage, and the confidence and personal dignity to maintain his composure in the face of great adversity.

That man was Jackie Robinson. Rickey and Robinson broke baseball's color barrier. Other black players, including Paige, who finally made it to the big leagues in 1948, benefited from this. Paige, Robinson, and many other men who had been denied their dream for so long finally had the chance to play in the major leagues. As a result, many of the greatest players in major league baseball—including men like Hank Aaron, Willie Mays, Ernie Banks, and Frank Robinson—were African Americans.

The lives of Paige, Robinson, and Rickey were connected by a string of milestones, each one made possible by the one before. Paige's natural ability on the pitcher's mound showed Rickey that black ballplayers were an untapped pool of talent. It was time to open the door to them. Rickey found Robinson's intense determination to succeed to be exactly the kind of quality he needed to successfully break baseball's color barrier. Robinson would further use this determination to help make strides in the cause of civil rights, which benefited the entire country. His breaking of baseball's color barrier helped lead the way for racial desegregation in the United States.

This was not an easy journey, but the impact of the collective accomplishments of Paige, Robinson, and Rickey helped shape the future of the United States—and the world. The color barrier was broken, and the civil rights movement had begun. As Satchel Paige might say, there was no looking back. ■

Satchel Paige (1906–1982)

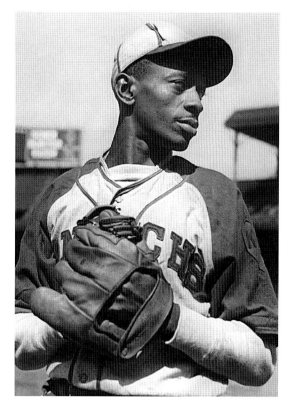

"Don't look back. Something might be gaining on you."[1] Satchel Paige spoke those words as part of his life's philosophy, and the words made up one of his most well-known sayings. If there was one thing that Paige really believed in his lifetime, it was that a person should always look forward. As one of the most famous players in the Negro leagues, Paige had long looked forward to the day when he would be able to pitch in baseball's major leagues. (A baseball league is an association of baseball clubs or teams. The major leagues consist of the two chief leagues of professional baseball in the United States, the National League and the American League.)

Many of the men who played in the major leagues believed that Paige was certainly good enough to join them in the big leagues. However, during nearly all the years of Paige's baseball career, racial *segregation*—that is, the separation of races, primarily black people from white people, by custom and at times even by law—was widespread in the United States. For example, black people were not allowed to eat in some restaurants and might be forced to use separate drinking fountains or separate public toilet facilities. There was also an unwritten rule that prevented blacks and whites from playing on the same baseball team.

In 1947, Brooklyn Dodgers team owner Branch Rickey signed African American player Jackie Robinson to the all-white team, finally breaking the color barrier of major league baseball. Although Satchel Paige did not become the first African American to play in the major leagues, he did realize his dream of pitching in the majors. In 1948, at age 42, he was signed by team owner Bill Veeck to play with the Cleveland (Ohio) Indians. Many of the players who got the opportunity to watch Paige in action thought that he was one of the best pitchers ever to play baseball. Most baseball fans continue to believe this today.

A RESTLESS CHILDHOOD

Leroy Robert Page was born in Mobile, Alabama, on July 7, 1906. He was the seventh of 12 children born to John and Lula Page. The family had little money. They lived in a small house in a poor section of Mobile. Satchel's father often found work as a gardener around town. Satchel's mother did the laundry of other people in the neighborhood so that her family would have money to buy food and clothing. When Satchel was born, the family spelled their last name "Page," but the family members later changed the spelling to "Paige." Satchel Paige once explained that his family changed the name's spelling "to make themselves sound more high-toned."[2]

As a boy, Paige did not like school—except when he was playing on the baseball team. He preferred to spend his time playing sandlot baseball. (Sandlot baseball is a type of baseball game played between informally organized teams, as on undeveloped city lots and small fields.) Paige often found himself in trouble with adults for misbehaving. Such misbehavior usually came in the form of skipping school and throwing rocks—sometimes at other children in the neighborhood.

Despite Paige's restless streak, even as a child he tried to earn money so that he could help support his family. Sometimes he would earn money by collecting and selling empty bottles. His most common source of income was carrying *satchels*, or bags, for travelers at the Mobile railroad depot. People started calling him "Satchel" Paige, and the name stuck. Some people said this work helped strengthen what would later become his pitching arm.

One day in 1918, when Paige was 12 years old, he made a mistake that changed his life. While walking past a local store window, he saw a bright display in the window. He went inside and took a handful of rings without paying for them. The man who owned the store caught him and took him to the police station.

Because Leroy had broken the law, and because he had gotten into mischief before, the court authorities decided that he had to be taught a lesson. On July 24, 1918, Paige was sentenced to the Industrial School for Negro Children in Mount Miegs, Alabama. This school was a *reformatory,* a correctional institution for young people who have committed minor crimes. By 1900, reformatories had been established throughout the United States. These institutions attempted to reform and educate youths rather than punish them. Reformatories provided counseling, education, vocational training, and other improvement programs.

Paige was terrified to leave his family. He never before had been away from home. He had to live at the school for more than five years. During that time, however, he was guaranteed something to eat and clothes to wear. He also received an education, something that many children from low-income families in the South were unable to do in the early 1900's. "I learned a lot of stuff. If they make you go where learning is flying around, some of it is bound to light on you,"[3] he once said.

Besides receiving an education in the classroom, Paige learned about something else that would forever change his life—how to play organized baseball. The baseball coach believed that Paige had a natural ability to pitch. It was as if Paige was born to be a baseball player. While at the school, the baseball coach taught him how to gain control over a baseball and master different pitches. Paige also learned how to study a batter. He studied the way the batter stood, positioned his body, or held a bat, so that, as the pitcher, he could throw a ball that the batter could not hit. His coach at the school encouraged Paige to become the best ballplayer he could be.

FROM CHILD'S PLAY TO SEMIPRO

In December 1923, the 17-year-old Paige was told he could return home to Mobile. At 6 feet, 3 ½ inches tall and 140 pounds, he was a tall, skinny teen-ager who looked more like a basketball player than a baseball player. His mother wanted her son to find a job to help support the family. His brothers and sisters were scraping together whatever money they could earn from various jobs around town, and the family wanted Paige to contribute. However, most of the business owners in Mobile knew Paige had been in a reformatory, and they feared he would continue to get in trouble.

By the spring of 1924, Paige was still looking for a way to make money. One day, he went to the local park where the Mobile Tigers practiced. The Tigers were an all-black semiprofessional baseball team. Wilson Paige, Satchel's older brother, played as both a pitcher and catcher for the Tigers. Paige told the manager he wanted to try out for the team. However, the manager was not sure this was a good idea. He had never seen Paige pitch and did not want to waste his time. But when Paige said he was Wilson's brother, the manager decided to see what this tall, gangly teen could do.

As he watched Paige, the manager could not believe his eyes. He let Paige throw 10 pitches. The manager stood at the plate with a bat but could not hit a single pitch. He told Paige to report with Wilson to play as a Mobile Tiger in the team's next game. "That was the point where I gave up kid's baseball . . . and started baseball as a career,"[4] Paige once said.

Paige was now making at least a little money doing what he wanted to do. In 1924, members of the team earned about $1 (about $11.50 today) a game—if enough fans showed up that day to watch them play. If the stands were empty, then all the players received was some lemonade to take home. Paige stayed with the Mobile Tigers through the 1925 season. He later claimed to have had a record of 30 wins and 1 loss in the 1924 season.

Sometimes, when the Tigers had a day off, Paige would get other teams in the area to pay him to pitch a game for them. This gave him and his family a little extra money, but he needed even more to support his family.

In the 1920's, there were many other semiprofessional and professional baseball teams playing in Alabama. Among the teams was one called the Mobile Bears. The Mobile Bears were an all-white minor league baseball team, and Paige knew that because of segregation, he would not be allowed to play for them. However, he had another idea. Paige went to work as a custodian at the field where the Bears practiced. After watching the white players, Paige decided he was as gifted a pitcher as anyone he saw on the mound. One day, several Bears players who had heard he was a pitcher challenged him to prove his stuff. Just as he did when he tried out for the Tigers, Paige struck out every batter who came to the plate.

Then the ugly reality of segregation reared its head. As the Bears walked off the field in amazement, one of them mentioned to Satchel that the team could really use a player like him—if only he were white.

Such comments upset Paige. He was clearly just as good (or even better) a ballplayer as anyone else—white or black. Paige later said this was the first time he heard that particular comment. He would hear it many times in the years to come. For the time being, all he could do was continue to practice at becoming a better pitcher for the all-black teams.

PLAYING IN THE NEGRO LEAGUES

Paige's practice paid off, and by 1926 he was pitching for the Down the Bay Boys, another baseball team from Mobile. Halfway through the 1926 season (after winning about 25 games), a friend asked Paige if he would like to pitch for a team in Tennessee called the Chattanooga Black Lookouts. The Black Lookouts were a professional baseball team affiliated with the Negro Southern League. Paige would be paid $50 (about $575 today) a month if he agreed. This was quite a pay increase from $1 or less a game. Paige jumped at the chance. Things were looking up for the young ballplayer.

From the late 1800's to the mid-1940's, black ballplayers were not allowed in the major leagues, so a number of Negro teams and leagues were organized. The term "Negro leagues" refers to this collection of leagues. The term also can refer more broadly to all Negro teams, including many that never belonged to a league.

Andrew "Rube" Foster, who began to pitch for a semiprofessional team in 1898 and later became a manager and owner, created the first successful Negro league, the Negro National League, in 1920. Competition among Negro ball clubs lasted until the mid-1960's, though, by then, most of the best black ballplayers were playing in the major leagues. The players of the Negro leagues collected a salary and played a regular schedule, just like their white counterparts in the major leagues. Yet, the Negro leagues received much less publicity than the major leagues—even during the height of their popularity from the 1920's through the 1940's.

Paige disliked unfair treatment by the managers and owners of ball clubs—regardless of whether those men were black or white.

Baseball was not always segregated. After the American Civil War (1861–1865), many talented African Americans showed that they were skilled baseball players and joined the same teams as white players. In the 1880's, some states, particularly in the southern United States, passed laws that required whites and blacks to be separated in many public places. Such attitudes also affected baseball. In 1887, the team owners of the International League, a prominent minor league, voted to ban all future contracts with African American players. This practice spread and, within a few years, those black players who had already been playing on International League or major league teams were dropped from the clubs.

The two major leagues that exist today—the National League, formed in 1876, and the American League, formed in 1901—had no written rules regarding segregation, but there was an "unwritten rule" prohibiting whites and blacks from being teammates. This unwritten rule, or understanding, would last until 1947.

Kenesaw Mountain Landis, an American judge who was appointed the first commissioner of professional baseball by club owners in 1920, and served until his death in 1944, steadfastly denied there was a color barrier—formal or informal—in organized baseball. Most baseball historians, however, view Landis as a major obstacle to baseball's integration. In 1947, three years after

Landis's death, the color barrier finally was broken, thanks to the efforts of Branch Rickey.

The color barrier notwithstanding, the Negro leagues included some outstanding talent. Hall of Fame baseball players such as Paige and Jackie Robinson, who, in 1947, became the first African American to play in the modern major leagues, both played in the Negro leagues. (The Baseball Hall of Fame, which opened in 1939, honors individuals who have made significant contributions to baseball. It is in Cooperstown, New York.) Legendary players such as Hank Aaron, Ernie Banks, James "Cool Papa" Bell, Roy Campanella, Josh Gibson, and Willie Mays also played in the Negro leagues. Many of these men went on to follow the groundbreaking footsteps of Jackie Robinson and play major league baseball. But others, such as Bell and Gibson, never got the chance to play in the majors because of their skin color. Some of these great players were no longer playing or had died by the time the game became *integrated* (available to people of all races on an equal basis).

Playing in the Negro leagues was difficult, even for a star like Satchel Paige. Black players often traveled from town to town in an old car or bus. When the team arrived in town, the players would hope to find a "blacks only" hotel where they could spend the night. Many times the black athletes had to sleep on the bus, the ground of the playing field, or even on the field's benches because the "whites only" hotels in town were off limits to them. Sometimes, the black players would stay with black families who lived in the area.

Paige, of course, did not like being treated unfairly by prejudiced hotel proprietors. Nor did he like unfair treatment by the managers and owners of ball clubs—regardless of whether those men were black or white. Many owners of Negro teams found it difficult to make a profit. But even those making large profits often paid low wages, especially compared with the white leagues. Negro team owners were notorious for dropping players or trying to steal good players from other teams. Most players, in return, were quick to jump to other teams for a better paycheck.

By the end of the 1926 season, Paige had become a star pitcher. Although he was only 20 years old, he was much better than many of his teammates who had been practicing and playing for nearly as long as he had been alive.

For this reason, Satchel Paige was willing to play baseball for whatever team would pay him the most money. Late in the 1926 season, he switched to the New Orleans Black Pelicans in Louisiana when they promised him a car along with $85 (about $935 today) a month. He returned to the Black Lookouts to start the 1927 season when that club agreed to pay him $200 (about $2,200 today) a month—a good salary for anyone in the 1920's.

MAKING THE "BIG LEAGUES"

Paige continued to seek a higher salary. A few games into the 1927 season, he signed a contract to play with the Birmingham Black Barons, a Negro league team in Alabama. The owner of the Black Barons paid Paige $275 (about $3,080 today) a month. For an African American player in the 1920's, this meant Paige had made it to the "big leagues." Just as he did when he played for the Tigers, Paige earned extra money by pitching for other teams whenever the Black Barons did not have a game scheduled.

Newspapers, most of them controlled by white owners, reported on Negro league games unevenly. In some cities, papers reported the games regularly, and in others, not at all. Yet word began to spread of Paige's prowess on the pitcher's mound. The Black Barons were one of the most popular Negro league teams of the era, and the addition of Paige to the roster further bolstered fan support over the next several years. He was the perfect combination of showmanship and sportsmanship.

"Everyone in the South knew about Satchel Paige . . . We'd have 8,000 people out—sometimes more—when he was pitching, which was something in Birmingham,"[5] teammate Jimmie Crutchfield once recalled.

Paige played with the Black Barons through most of the 1930 season, switching for a short time to the Black Sox of Baltimore.

He found himself on the move again in 1931, when he agreed to join the Elite Giants of Nashville, Tennessee, and he stayed with the team when it moved to Ohio and became the Cleveland Cubs. His allegiance did not last long, though. In June 1931, Paige was on the mound as a member of the Pittsburgh (Pennsylvania) Crawfords.

The Crawfords were one of the most successful teams in Negro league history. Because of the large African American population in Pittsburgh, Negro league baseball thrived in the city. The game was so popular in Pittsburgh that it boasted two hometown teams—the Crawfords and the rival Homestead Grays.

With the addition of Paige, the Pittsburgh Crawfords' roster included—at one point or another—such notable players (and future Hall of Famers) as Bell, Gibson, Oscar Charleston, and Judy Johnson. Many baseball historians consider Paige and Josh Gibson (who played for the Crawfords from 1932 to 1936) as the most dominant pitcher-catcher combination ever to play the game of baseball—in any league.

Paige talks with his wife, Janet, in 1941, when he was a player with the Kansas City Monarchs. The couple married in 1934.

Paige's 1934 season with the Crawfords was his most successful. Over the course of 20 recorded league games that season, he allowed only 85 hits in 154 innings pitched. He also achieved 97 strikeouts. In addition, he won the Negro leagues' annual East-West All-Star Game, an event on par with major league baseball's All-Star Game today.

PERSONAL CHANGES, PROFESSIONAL CHALLENGES

During the final month of the 1934 season, Paige played for a semiprofessional team in North Dakota called the Bismarck Baseball Club. Many of his teammates (who were white) were not fond of Paige's boasting that he was better than they were. However, Paige brought the team victories and publicity. In October 1934, he led the first of several squads of Negro league players in postseason exhibition games against their white major league counterparts.

On Oct. 26, 1934, Paige married Janet Howard, a waitress whom the baseball star met shortly after his arrival in Pittsburgh. Almost from the start, married life proved to be a problem for Paige and his bride.

The couple honeymooned in California. While there, Paige also played exhibition baseball games, including an exciting 13-inning, 1-to-0 win against pitcher Dizzy Dean of the major league St. Louis Cardinals. As a result of this and other exhibition games, many major league players, including Dean, Joe DiMaggio of the New York Yankees, Charlie Gehringer of the Detroit Tigers, and Ted Williams of the Boston Red Sox, called Paige the best pitcher—white or black—whom they had ever seen. Among those who also witnessed Paige's ability was a man named Bill Veeck *(vehk)*, who 13 years later would play a pivotal role in changing Paige's life.

In 1935, the owner of the Crawfords refused to match the pay offered by Bismarck, so Paige returned to the North Dakota team for a highly successful season. While in the Midwest, Paige occasionally joined the Kansas City Monarchs to pitch. Throughout the 1930's and into the 1940's, Paige and several other Negro league players earned extra money by playing baseball outside the United States during the winter months. Traveling to the Caribbean, Mexico, and South America, they would "play-for-pay"— that is, they were paid per game or for a limited period—before returning to their assigned Negro league teams. One of Paige's best traveling years was 1939 in Puerto Rico, in which he had a 1.93 *earned-run average (ERA)*. Earned-run average is the average of *earned runs* scored against a pitcher every nine innings. An earned run is a run that is scored without the aid of an error.

In 1936, Paige accepted a new offer to pitch again for the Crawfords, but by 1937 he had decided to leave Negro league baseball and play in the Dominican Republic for that country's president, Rafael Trujillo Molina. Trujillo was a big baseball fan and closely associated with Los Dragones ("the Dragons"), the team of the Dominican national capital. This team was competing for wins and prestige with teams supported by Trujillo's political rivals. Trujillo hired the best Negro league players from the United States to join outstanding players from the Caribbean region on Los Dragones. Paige was paid $6,000 (about $81,000 today) to play for the team, while such other stars as Bell and Gibson were paid $3,000 (about $40,500 today) each.

Armed soldiers guarded the exits during many of the games to protect the players. At one point, the players were even placed in jail so that they would not be able to go out in the evenings to enjoy the nightlife. When Los Dragones lost a game, the president announced that it was not to happen again. After Los Dragones won the Dominican league championship game, Paige and his teammates quickly left the Dominican Republic.

When Paige returned to the United States, he learned that the Negro league owners had barred him and a number of other players from playing for any of their teams because these players had

Paige warms up his pitching arm before a Negro league game between the Kansas City Monarchs and the New York Cuban Stars. The game was played at Yankee Stadium in New York City.

left the U.S. teams at the start of the summer season to play in Latin America. Not to be defeated, he spent the remainder of 1937 touring the United States with a group of players who became known as the Satchel Paige All-Stars. In 1938, league owners readmitted Paige and sold his contract to the Newark Eagles in New Jersey. Money became an issue in the negotiation process, and Paige instead announced plans to play baseball in the Mexican League.

Soon after he arrived in Mexico, Paige, who had always taken great pains to protect his pitching arm, complained of soreness in his arm. Physicians examined Paige's arm and declared that his pitching career was over.

Returning to the United States, Paige began to struggle with financial difficulties and was unable to find work in baseball—not even as a manager or coach. He had to sell some of the possessions he had worked so long and hard to buy. Then, he signed a contract with the Kansas City Monarchs in Missouri. That team's owners believed that fans would still want to see him pitch, if only for an inning or two.

During 1939 and much of 1940, Paige toured with the Monarch's "second" team. At first, his arm was not in good enough shape to play with the Monarch's main team. But eventually, his arm improved, and Paige developed a devastating curve ball to add to his arsenal of pitches. In 1940, he moved to the main Monarchs team, proving that his career was far from over.

Paige helped the Monarchs win Negro American League *pennants* (championships) in 1940, 1941, 1942, and 1946. When the Monarchs swept the 1942 Negro League World Series by defeating the Homestead Grays in four straight games, Paige was the starting pitcher for three of those games.

As a ballplayer, Paige was rarely at home and spent little time with his wife, Janet. Even before he left to play in Mexico, he and his wife rarely saw one another. He had trouble settling down in the role of a married man, and the couple divorced in 1943.

Satchel did not let his personal problems get in the way of playing baseball. While a member of the Monarchs, he would also "loan" himself to such independent ball clubs and Negro league teams as the New York Black Yankees, the Memphis Red Sox, and the Philadelphia Stars. In addition, he gathered another group of Negro league players at the end of the 1946 season to take on the Bob Feller All-Stars, a team led by major league pitcher Bob Feller of the Cleveland Indians. Facing white players again, Paige held his own, just as he had against Dizzy Dean and his compatriots in 1934. Paige and Feller faced off with opposing All-Star teams again in 1947.

Along the way, Paige also found love again, with a woman named Lahoma Brown. The couple married on Oct. 12, 1947. They raised Lahoma's daughter, Shirley, and had seven more children: Pamela Jean, Carolyn Lahoma, Linda Sue, Robert LeRoy, Lula Ouida, Rita Jean, and Warren James.

Paige estimated that during his career he started some 2,600 games and amassed 2,000 wins, 300 shut-outs, and 55 no-hitters.

In 1947, Paige was over 40 years old—an age at which most ballplayers are considering retirement. For several years, however, Paige had other ideas in mind. He wanted to become the first African American to play in the major leagues. He knew that there were, without question, many talented black ballplayers, but he believed (and few had the courage to argue with him) that he was the best. Furthermore, Paige correctly argued that he was still a big draw at the game ticket window—many people would pay to attend Negro league games simply to watch Paige pitch.

Statistics from most Negro league games are difficult to verify, since there was little record-keeping—and those records that were kept were often inaccurate. However, Paige estimated that during his career he started some 2,600 games and amassed 2,000 wins, 300 *shut-outs* (games in which the opposing team is kept from scoring), and 55 *no-hitters* (games in which the pitcher gives up no base hits to the opposing team). In comparison, any modern-day pitcher who wins 300 major league games is almost certain to be elected to the Baseball Hall of Fame. The greatest white pitcher in the annals of professional baseball, Cy Young, won 511 major league games in a career that stretched from 1890 through 1911. Nolan Ryan holds the major league record for no-hitters, with seven between 1966 and 1993.

THE OLDEST ROOKIE IN THE MAJORS

Paige correctly predicted that the day was coming when the unwritten rule barring blacks from playing alongside whites would be broken. As early as 1943, Bill Veeck, a minor league executive, had an idea to buy the major league Philadelphia Phillies in Pennsylvania and then obtain the contracts of Paige and other Negro league legends to play on the team. Instead, the owner of the Phillies sold the team to someone else, and Veeck opted to buy the Cleveland Indians in Ohio. But Veeck never forgot about Paige.

In October 1945, Jackie Robinson, who had been one of Paige's teammates on the Monarchs, signed a contract with the Montreal Royals, a Canadian minor league affiliate of the National League's Brooklyn Dodgers. Robinson joined the Royals in 1946, helping the team to dominate the International League. On April 10, 1947, Branch Rickey, the owner of the Dodgers, purchased Robinson's contract and, on April 15, Robinson became the first African American athlete to play modern major league baseball.

Paige viewed this news with mixed emotions. He praised Robinson and his abilities as a ballplayer, and he joked with one reporter that major league baseball did not ask him because "my price is too high."[6] He was disappointed that the opportunity had not fallen to him, yet he realized that Robinson opened a door that had remained closed to him and other Negro leaguers for decades.

With the integration of baseball now slowly underway, the American League was poised to follow in the footsteps of the National League. Four years after his aborted plan to stock a major league team with Negro league players, Bill Veeck was ready to sign a black player to the American League's Cleveland Indians.

Paige pitched for the Cleveland Indians in 1948, his first year in the major leagues.

Veeck considered signing Paige, but in the end decided against it. The stakes were too high, and Veeck felt that some people would view his signing of the aging pitcher as little more than a publicity stunt. Veeck was no stranger to publicity during his career, however. As one of the most successful and creative owners in history, his imaginative promotions were well known. These included fireworks at ballgames and the first "exploding" scoreboard, which let off rockets, sirens, and blazing lights whenever the home team hit a home run.

For the first black player in the American League, Veeck selected Larry Doby, a star player with the Newark Eagles, on July 5, 1947. At 23, Doby was considerably younger than the 41-year-old Paige. Paige sent Veeck a telegram and asked if the maverick owner would ever consider signing him to a playing contract. "All things in due time,"[7] Veeck replied.

Down but not out, Paige started out the 1948 season with the Monarchs. On July 7, 1948, the day came that he had been waiting for. It was on this day—Paige's 42nd birthday—that Veeck invited him to try out for the Cleveland Indians. As owner of the Indians, it was certainly Veeck's right to extend such an invitation, but Lou Boudreau, who was the team's field manager, was not convinced of the wisdom of Veeck's move.

When Boudreau tried to hit Paige's pitches, however, he struck out nearly every time. Then, when Boudreau caught Paige's pitches, each ball was directly on target. Boudreau was amazed, and admitted that Paige would be a powerful addition to the ball club.

Despite Paige's impressive statistics, some baseball purists claimed that Veeck was making a mockery of the game by signing "the oldest rookie." They and others maintained that bringing the well-known Negro league pitcher into the Indians organization was merely a publicity stunt. In response, Paige compiled a 6-1 record with a 2.48 ERA (despite his late start in the season), pitching alongside his former all-star opponent, Bob Feller. In the first three games in which Paige was the starting pitcher, 200,000 people saw him pitch. He also helped the Indians win several "must-win" games, which helped the team to capture the 1948 American League pennant and the World Series.

BASEBALL VETERAN

Veeck decided to sell the Indians after the 1949 season, and the new owners opted to release Paige because they thought the legendary pitcher was now too old to play in the majors. Paige then played with the Monarchs and the Philadelphia Stars of the Negro leagues. But when Veeck purchased the St. Louis Browns in the summer of 1951, he quickly signed Paige and added him to the team's pitching rotation.

Playing for the 1951 Browns, Paige won three and lost four games, posting an ERA of 4.79. The following year, he won 12 games, and his ERA was 3.07. In 1952 and 1953, he was named to the American League squad for the All-Star game. In 1953, Veeck sold the Browns and, again, the new ownership decided to relocate, renaming the team the Baltimore Orioles. The ownership also decided that they did not want Paige on their team, again because of his age.

The ageless wonder took the "age" issue in stride: "Age is a question of mind over matter," he said. "If you don't mind, it doesn't matter."[8]

Paige's overall record in the major leagues stood at 28 wins and 31 losses, with 32 saves and a 3.29 ERA.

Between 1954 and 1956, Paige moved from team to team in the Negro leagues, including another stint with the Monarchs. Fans still adored Paige and were happy to see the Negro league and major league icon take the mound.

In 1956, Veeck, who had founded the Miami (Florida) Marlins of the International League, invited Paige to become a minor league pitcher. As a stunt, Paige was delivered to the playing field in a helicopter for the first game after his signing. During his first scheduled start, he tossed a four-hit shutout against the defending champion Montreal Royals.

> *"Age is a question of mind over matter. If you don't mind, it doesn't matter."*
>
> Satchel Paige

Paige continued to play with the Marlins through the end of the 1958 season. In addition, he took a small role as an army sergeant in the motion picture *The Wonderful Country* (1959), a western starring Robert Mitchum and Julie London. Until 1965, Paige was a type of baseball curiosity, touring the United States with various teams, including the Monarchs and the Portland Beavers of the Pacific Coast League.

In 1965, Paige, 59, met with Charles O. Finley, owner of the major league Kansas City Athletics (A's). The A's were in the midst of a terrible season and Finley, in a bid to spur fan interest, created a series of "Novelty Nights." On Sept. 25, 1965, Paige took to the mound in an Athletics' uniform for a game against the Boston Red Sox. In three innings of play, he allowed one hit (a *double* [a hit in which a batter gets to second base] to Carl Yastrzemski) and then retired the remaining batters with an impressive array of expertly controlled pitches. This was Paige's

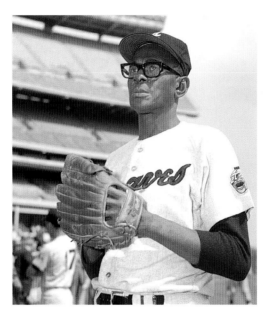

Paige wears the uniform of the Atlanta Braves in 1968. The team signed the legendary pitcher, who was over 60 years old at the time, as a player-coach, but he would never pitch a game with them.

final major league appearance.

In 1966 and 1967, Paige played with a few minor league teams, as well as with the Negro leagues' Indianapolis Clowns.

After facing the injustice of not being able to play in the major leagues because of segregation, Paige faced another injustice at the hands of major league baseball—he was ineligible for a league pension. To qualify for retirement benefits, a player had to have amassed five years of playing time on major league teams. In spite of a lifetime in baseball, Paige missed this mark by 158 days.

Veeck came to Paige's defense yet again, rallying for his cause. Although Veeck was no longer a team owner, he criticized those who did own teams for failing to help Paige. In August 1968, the Atlanta Braves signed Paige as a player-coach for the rest of that season and for 1969, thus qualifying him for benefits. Paige never tossed a single game pitch for the Braves and, in mid-1969, he announced his retirement from the game.

In 1971, Paige was inducted into the National Baseball Hall of Fame in Cooperstown, New York. He became the first player to be honored on the basis of his Negro league career. (Jackie Robinson was inducted into the Hall of Fame in 1962 based on the 10 years he played in the major leagues.)

Paige did not dwell on baseball's history of segregation when he was inducted into the Hall of Fame. But at a banquet later, he criticized the major league teams for having no African American managers. He also commented on why he thought capable Negro league players had been kept out of the major leagues for so long. An upset Hall of Fame press official asked Paige to sit down, and Paige complied. In his 1962 autobiography, *Maybe I'll Pitch Forever*, Paige discussed in detail the racism he had encountered in his life.

PAIGE'S FINAL INNINGS

In the late 1970's, Paige suffered from a heart ailment and emphysema. He was confined to a wheelchair and relied on a respirator to breathe. His love of baseball, however, never wavered. On June 5, 1982, he appeared at the dedication of a Kansas City stadium named in his honor and threw out the first pitch at a Little League game.

On June 8, 1982, Paige died. Following his death, many people noted that Paige had been deprived of playing alongside some of the best players in the game while he was in his prime. But Paige knew better. When he and his Negro league teammates squared off against their white major league opponents in exhibition games, it was usually the major leaguers who went home the losers. Paige had at least the personal satisfaction of knowing he was one of the world's best baseball players during his lifetime and that he was one of the sport's best-loved stars.

Baseball fans today continue to regard Paige as one of the greatest players in the history of the game. Indeed, Satchel Paige never need look back. ■

Chronology of Robinson's Life

1919	born on January 31 in Cairo, Georgia
1937	graduates from John Muir Technical School in Pasadena, California, where he stars in baseball, football, and track
1939	enrolls in University of California at Los Angeles, where he earns varsity letters in baseball, basketball, football, and track
1941	leaves college to play in minor league football for Honolulu (Hawaii) Bears
1942	drafted into United States Army
1943	becomes 2nd lieutenant assigned to African American truck battalion at Fort Riley, Kansas
1944	acquitted of charges of disrespect and disobedience by court-martial board; honorably discharged from army
1945	joins Kansas City (Missouri) Monarchs, Negro league baseball team
1946	marries Rachel Isum on February 10
1947	joins Brooklyn Dodgers as first African American to play in modern major league baseball
1949	voted to play in his first All-Star Game; wins National League batting title and most valuable player award; leads major leagues in stolen bases
1956	retires from baseball; awarded Spingarn Medal
1957	becomes active in National Association for the Advancement of Colored People (NAACP)
1962	elected into National Baseball Hall of Fame
1966	appointed as special assistant for community affairs to governor of New York State
1972	invited by Jesse Jackson to serve as first vice president of People United to Save Humanity (PUSH); dies of heart attack at home in Stamford, Connecticut, on October 24

Jackie Robinson (1919–1972)

Throughout his lifetime, Jackie Robinson gave "110 percent" to everything he did. When it came to confronting racial inequality, he gave 110 percent. The same can be said of his service as an officer in the United States Army during World War II (1939–1945). When Jackie Robinson was chosen in 1947 by Brooklyn Dodgers general manager Branch Rickey to be the first African American to play modern major league baseball, Robinson again gave 110 percent. Whether it was in sports, the military, or the civil rights movement, Jackie Robinson always went above and beyond the call to do what he believed was right.

In the early part of the 1900's, discrimination based on race was common in the United States. Black Americans were often treated unfairly. It was into such a world that Jack Roosevelt Robinson was born on Jan. 31, 1919, in Cairo, Georgia. His parents, Jerry and Mallie Robinson, already had three sons and a daughter by the time Jackie (as he was to be called) came along.

Jerry and Mallie Robinson married in 1909. Originally, Jerry Robinson worked on farms and was paid $12 (about $260 today) a month. Eventually, the Robinsons became *sharecroppers*—that is, they farmed a section of land owned by another person. In return, they kept a portion of the crop and whatever money came from its sale. This was more money than the family had been making, but it was still not an easy life for them.

As a child, Jackie heard stories about the experiences of his mother's parents, who both had been slaves. By the 1920's, life remained very difficult for many black Americans. As sharecroppers, the Robinson family had to buy their own seeds and equipment from the farm owner. Like most sharecroppers at that time, they also lived in a house that belonged to the farm owner. If the Robinsons did not have enough money, they would have to use credit to buy what they needed and then repay the owner when they received money from the crop sales.

For many sharecroppers, the cost of planting and caring for the crops totalled more than the amount of money they made at the end of the season. As a result, they owed a great deal of money and had to try to repay it during the next growing season, often with the addition of high interest. This dilemma faced them year after year, with many black sharecropper families never finding a way to get out of debt.

The pressures of sharecropping caused much stress in the lives of black families. Sometimes, it was more stress than families could handle. This is what happened to Jackie Robinson's family. When Jackie was only about 6 months old, his father gave up on this way of life. He told his wife that he was going to Texas to visit some of his relatives. In reality, he had grown tired of the difficult work involved in sharecropping and being the head of a family. He decided to leave everything behind. He had also fallen in love with the wife of a neighbor, and the two decided to run away together.

When the family discovered what had happened, they were uncertain about what to do. Mallie Robinson was a hard worker, but she could not take care of a farm with only young children to help her. Living in Georgia was the only life Mallie had ever known, but she concluded she could no longer support her family there.

Mallie had a half-brother who lived in Pasadena, California. She packed up everything she owned and, with her children—Edgar, Frank, Mack, Willa Mae, and Jackie—got on a train that took them to Pasadena. At the same time, Mallie's sister and brother-in-law, Cora and Sam Wade, went to California with their two children.

The Robinson family soon learned that living in California was very different than living in Georgia. For a while, Mallie and Cora and their families lived with their brother at his house. Mallie took jobs cooking and cleaning for white families in town. It was difficult, exhausting work, and she had to spend hours away from her children. Some weeks, she had barely enough money to feed her family. But there were also days when she was able to bring leftover food from her job home for her family. In addition, whatever money Mallie earned was always hers to keep. She did not have to share it with a farm owner, as she had to do in Georgia. More importantly, she was able to begin saving some money, so that one day her family could afford the things they needed.

Many years later, Jackie would recall that, although he was very young at the time, he was aware of how hard his mother had to work. He also recalled how she found time to give her children the attention and love that they needed. Robinson would acknowledge that it was his mother who instilled in him the importance of dedication, hard work, and loyalty.

Jackie felt especially close to his older sister, Willa Mae. When Jackie was still too young to go to school, his mother would have his older sister watch over him while she went to work. For Willa Mae, watching over Jackie included taking him to school with her. The teacher told Mallie it would be all right if Willa Mae brought her little brother to school, but he would have to play in the sandbox outside during class. (If it rained, the teacher would let him sit quietly in the classroom.) That was fine with Jackie.

Chapter 1: Experiencing Racial Intolerance

Willa Mae tried to protect her younger brother from racial intolerance, but this was not always possible. Jackie's mother warned him that some people would not like him simply because of the color of his skin. He would always credit his mother with teaching him and his siblings how to deal with people who were *racist*—that is, people who disliked the family just because they were black.

In 1922, for example, Mallie and the Wades were able to save enough money to buy a house together in a mostly white area of Pasadena. Two years later, the Wades moved into another house nearby. Many of the neighbors were unhappy that black families were living in their neighborhood.

One day Jackie was outside the house doing his chores when a neighborhood girl, who was white, walked past and shouted a racist insult at him. Robinson responded by calling her a name. The girl's father became angry at the little boy when he heard this and came outside. Robinson would later tell the story of how he and the man got into a rock-throwing fight before someone made them stop.

That incident was Robinson's first personal experience with racial intolerance, but it was not the first—or last—problem his family encountered regarding racism. Other neighbors in Pasadena would sometimes call the police if one of the Robinson boys made too much noise. When the Robinsons had purchased their house, several neighbors started a petition to get them to move out of the neighborhood. Someone even burned a cross on their front lawn. (Cross burning was a practice intended to frighten people, because it commonly was used as a threat or warning by the Ku Klux Klan, a group of white secret societies who oppose the advancement of blacks, Jews, and other minority groups.) Despite this threatening act, the family would not be intimidated. They liked where they lived, and they refused to move out of the neighborhood.

Other families in the neighborhood took note of the Robinson's courage. Over time, the area became a mix of white, black, Asian, and Hispanic families. Robinson's family had, in effect, broken the neighborhood's color barrier.

When he was old enough, Robinson joined his brothers and sister as a student at school. He first attended Cleveland Elementary School and later Washington Elementary School, both in Pasadena. At both schools, Robinson was an average student. However, he excelled at sports. People often commented on the young boy's athletic ability. As with Leroy "Satchel" Paige, who was a famous pitcher in the Negro leagues at the time, it was almost as if Robinson were born to play sports.

When Robinson was 10 years old, the United States began to suffer the effects of the *Great Depression,* a period of economic hardship that began in 1929 and lasted throughout the 1930's. The family never had a lot of money, and now the siutation was even more financially challenging. Robinson tried to earn extra money for the family by selling newspapers or doing yard work for neighbors. Sometimes, he would sell hot dogs at football games at the nearby Rose Bowl Stadium.

Although his mother tried to be a strong influence on him, the teen-age Robinson and other boys would sometimes get into mischief by throwing things at passing cars or stealing fruit from the local grocery store. Robinson usually avoided serious trouble, though, thanks to his mother's guidance. She had worked hard to instill certain values in him, and he did not want to disappoint her.

Robinson enjoyed channeling his energy into sports. On most days, he would spend time at the local park playing baseball. (On Sundays, however, his mother was often upset that he was not spending that time attending church services.) After graduating from Washington Junior High School in 1935, Robinson enrolled in John Muir Technical School. He participated in every sport the school offered, and he was soon a star in several sports. Before graduation, he *lettered* in baseball, basketball, football, and track. (A sports letter is the initial of a school, college, or other institution given as an award or trophy to members of a sports team.)

BROTHERS IN ATHLETICS

Athleticism ran in the Robinson family. While Jackie was excelling at high school sports, his oldest brother, Edgar, had a reputation around town as being the fastest boy on a bicycle or roller-skates. Another brother, Mack, was a runner who won the chance to represent the United States in the 1936 Summer Olympic Games in track and field.

The 1936 Olympics were held in Berlin, Germany. Before the games were held, Germany's Nazi dictator, Adolf Hitler, had boasted that the games would prove that "Aryans"—a term the Nazis used for many Germans and certain other peoples of northern Europe—were superior to all other peoples. However, the Nazis had not anticipated the talent of some of the members of the U.S. team, especially a runner named Jesse Owens. Owens, who was black, won four gold medals at the 1936 Olympics. The U.S. team's victory was a point of pride for Mack Robinson, who won a silver medal in the 200-meter race, bested only by Owens.

Jackie Robinson was awed and inspired by his brother's Olympic accomplishments. In 1937, upon graduation from high school, Robinson enrolled in Pasadena Junior College. While there, he continued to build upon his sports accomplishments. At the start of his first football season, he chipped a bone in his ankle during a practice game. It took weeks to heal, but when it did, he rushed back to the playing field and became *first-string* (starting line-up) quarterback.

People also marveled at Robinson's skills as a baseball and track star. One morning in May 1938, Robinson set a national junior college track record in the running broad jump. The record he broke had been set by his brother Mack. Robinson then hurried to a nearby town to play in an afternoon baseball game for the Pasadena Junior College team. He made several key plays to help the team win a vital game in its divisional playoffs.

UCLA: GLORY AND CHALLENGES

In 1939, Robinson decided to continue his education at the University of California at Los Angeles (UCLA), one of the many colleges and universities that had offered him an athletic scholarship. This school was close to Pasadena, so Robinson could still be near his family.

While attending UCLA, Robinson experienced several episodes of racial hatred. Sometimes white players on rival teams would deliberately foul him or insult and taunt him. Robinson and his friends also faced some incidents of name-calling and insults outside of school. Robinson got into trouble over these incidents a few times but, for the most part, he concentrated on his studies and sports and refused to be intimidated by taunts and other aggressive behavior.

This course of action paid off well for Robinson. He became the first student in UCLA history to earn varsity letters in four sports in the same year. Those sports were baseball, basketball, football, and track. He became the UCLA basketball team's leading scorer. As a member of the university's football team, he excelled in rushing and punt-return yards. He played halfback and safety on UCLA's unbeaten 1939 squad. In that season, the team posted a record of 6-0-4 (6 wins, 0 losses, 4 ties), including two scoreless ties.

Robinson went on to add even more athletic accomplishments to his name at UCLA. He was voted the best all-around athlete on the West Coast, and he led the Southern Division of the Pacific Coast Conference in basketball scoring twice. In addition, Robinson won the Pacific Coast Intercollegiate Golf Championship and once reached the National Negro Tennis Tournament Semifinals.

Although Robinson was an excellent athlete at UCLA, his grades were only average. He wanted to earn money to help support his mother and the rest of his family. Because of racial

American Jesse Owens competed in the 200-meter race at the 1936 Summer Olympic Games in Berlin, Germany. He won four gold medals for the U.S. team. Owens believed that athletic competition could help solve racial and political problems.

After starring in football at the University of California at Los Angeles, Jackie Robinson went on to play semiprofessional and minor league football.

discrimination, Robinson began to wonder what chance he would have of succeeding even with a college degree. In the spring of 1941, he decided to not finish college. Robinson once wrote that, at the time, he "was convinced that no amount of education would help a black man get a job."[1]

At first, he found work at a youth camp. Being a versatile athlete, he then decided that he would try his hand playing football for a professional team. However, there were no black players in the National Football League (the professional U.S. football league). Robinson earned extra money playing briefly for a semiprofessional football team called the Los Angeles Bulldogs. He eventually moved to Hawaii and played for a minor league football team called the Honolulu Bears. He also earned money working for a construction company not far from the military base at Pearl Harbor, on the island of Oahu in Hawaii.

Robinson enjoyed playing football, but Hawaii was a long way from California and he greatly missed his family. In November 1941, the Honolulu Bears finished their season. On December 5 of that year, a homesick Jackie Robinson packed up his things, got on a boat, and headed back to Pasadena. Two days later, on December 7, while Robinson was still at sea, he and the other passengers on his boat learned that Japanese ships and airplanes had launched a surprise military attack on the U.S. naval base at Pearl Harbor. The attack killed and injured many American sailors and soldiers. It also destroyed much of the U.S. Navy's Pacific Fleet.

The attack on Pearl Harbor forced the United States to enter World War II, which was already raging in much of the rest of the world.

Chapter 2: Lieutenant Robinson

The news of the Japanese attack on Pearl Harbor stunned people throughout the United States. Although the war had been going on in Europe and elsewhere for more than two years, leaders in the United States had been trying to avoid joining the conflict. All that was about to change—and quickly.

Four months after returning to California, Robinson received a notice that he had been expecting since he first heard about the attack on Pearl Harbor. He had been *drafted* into the United States Army. (A military draft is a system of selecting men for required military service.)

The U.S. Army ordered Robinson to report to Fort Riley, Kansas, for basic training. All new soldiers had to undergo basic training, in which they learned fundamental military skills. These skills included marksmanship, first aid, and navigation. Trainees underwent intense physical training and were taught to act as part of a disciplined team. Robinson's years of participation in team sports helped prepare him for these demands.

While stationed at Fort Riley, Robinson decided that he wanted to become an officer in the army. He applied for entry into Officers Candidate School (OCS). He was then required to take an entrance examination administered by the army to qualify for the OCS program. Robinson was excited to hear that he passed the test. He thought that, for one of the few times in his life, people were not judging him only by the color of his skin. His excitement, however, was short-lived.

After passing the test, Robinson waited for at least three months for orders on where he should report for OCS duty. He was not alone. Other African American men who had performed well on the entrance examination were also waiting for their assignments. Meanwhile, white soldiers had long ago received their orders for OCS training. Robinson, who had met all the requirements set by the army, began to wonder if the fact that he was black was playing a role in the delay.

Robinson served as 2nd lieutenant in the United States Army during World War II.

There was little that Robinson could do about the situation. Then, one day, a new soldier joined the ranks at Fort Riley. His name was Joe Louis. Louis was an African American boxer who had held the world heavyweight championship since 1937. Many Americans—both black and white—greatly admired Louis as a boxer.

Robinson informed Louis of his concern that he was not receiving assignments because of his race. Louis did not like to hear about racial injustice, and he made some phone calls to address Robinson's concern. Because he was a famous boxer, Louis had some important connections, including a few powerful contacts in the federal government in Washington, D.C. Before long, Robinson received word that he would be admitted into Fort Riley's OCS program.

CONFRONTING RACIAL INJUSTICE IN THE ARMY

Robinson graduated the OCS program as a 2nd lieutenant in January 1943. He was assigned to an African American truck battalion at Fort Riley as the battalion's morale officer. Morale, however, was low. The black soldiers were upset. They did not like the fact that even though they were willing to fight for their country, they were still being mistreated because of their race. For example, they told their new morale officer that there were only a few seats set aside for blacks in the company's snack bar, where they would sometimes eat. (The army was still segregated in the 1940's, so blacks and whites had to eat in separate areas.) If there were no available seats in the black section, the black soldiers were not allowed to join the white soldiers or to sit at empty tables reserved for "Whites Only." As a result, the soldiers often had to eat standing up.

Lieutenant Robinson took his job seriously and requested that his superiors make more room for blacks. It was not easy, but he continued to push hard for change and, eventually, more seats were made available for the black soldiers. Actions such as this caused the soldiers who worked for Robinson to greatly admire and respect him.

Not all of Robinson's efforts were as successful as his attempt to get extra seating for his troops. Robinson had to endure racial injustice in many other areas. For example, blacks were not allowed to play on Fort Riley's baseball team. Robinson was upset about this, but there was nothing he could do to change it.

The commander at Fort Riley, however, was a football fan and wanted his team to win. He knew that Robinson had played football in high school and college. He also knew that Robinson was one of the best players around. The commander invited Robinson to join the company's football team. Robinson was happy to be playing sports again. In the season's first game, the Fort Riley team was scheduled to play the football team from the University of Missouri. When the players and coaches of the opposing team learned that an African American was on the squad, they sent word that they would not take the field.

On short notice, Robinson was given a pass to take some time off and visit his family in California. He accepted the pass, but he suspected that the reason he received it was so that he would be out of town when his team played the University of Missouri.

American Joe Louis became the world heavyweight champion of boxing in 1937. Louis later served with Robinson in the army.

When he returned from his leave, Robinson told his commander that he was quitting the team and would refuse any offer to play for them again.

During the summer and fall of 1943, Robinson aggravated the ankle injury he had suffered while playing football at Pasadena Junior College. He was reassigned to limited duty. In the spring of 1944, he was assigned to a tank platoon stationed at Camp Hood in Texas, where he quickly gained the respect of his men. His commanding officer suggested that he consider requesting to go to Europe with his unit, despite his damaged ankle. Robinson agreed. However, he first had to have his ankle reexamined at a nearby hospital.

At the time, state and local governments could enact laws preventing African Americans from sitting in the same areas as whites. Although such segregation still existed in much of the United States, the army had made efforts to eliminate it by 1944. The army no longer forced African American servicemen to sit in the rear of buses when the vehicles picked them up on military bases.

One evening, Lieutenant Robinson boarded a bus on the base to return to the hospital where tests were being conducted on his ankle. He sat in the middle of the vehicle next to the wife of one of his friends. When the driver noticed this, he immediately told Robinson to move to the back of the bus. Robinson knew that the driver could not order him to do this, and so he refused to move. He had done nothing wrong. He knew his rights as a soldier, and he argued with the bus driver.

When the vehicle arrived at the base's central bus depot, there was an angry exchange of words between Robinson and the driver. The driver called military police to report Robinson, who was taken to the police captain. The captain outranked Robinson, but the lieutenant held his ground and again argued that he had not broken any law. The other officer did not like Robinson's attitude. In July 1944, the officer filed charges against him for disrespect and disobedience. The charges meant that Robinson would face a *court-martial,* a military court that tries members of the armed forces who are accused of committing certain crimes.

The disrespect and disobedience charges stemmed from Robinson's demeanor toward the military police officers, whom he felt had sympathized with the bus driver and not listened to his side of the argument. Robinson and his attorney argued their case before the court-martial board, noting that explicit racial slurs had been directed at Robinson, prompting his anger. The prosecuting attorneys provided ample evidence that Robinson was asked to move to the rear of the bus, and that he resisted the repeated demands of the driver.

After hearing the arguments made by both sides, the court-martial board determined that Robinson had done nothing wrong and cleared him of the charges. His army record would stay clean. The acquittal helped convince Robinson that if he acted in accordance with his conscience, he would ultimately be vindicated. That belief would later help him endure the abuse he received early in his career in the major leagues.

Although his acquittal was good news for the morale officer and it would eventually serve him well, the experience embittered Robinson. While he was defending himself at the trial, the rest of his unit was sent to Europe for duty. Robinson soon became disenchanted by life in the military. He had worked hard to become an army officer, but he was not getting the respect that white officers commonly received.

Following the trial, Robinson requested that he be discharged from the army because of his ankle injury. The army agreed, and on Nov. 28, 1944, 2nd Lieutenant Jack R. Robinson was honorably discharged from the U.S. Army. He returned to California and his family. In 1945, the United States and its Allies achieved victory and World War II was over.

RETURNING TO CIVILIAN LIFE

It was time for Robinson to resume his civilian life. Foremost in his mind was the resumption of his relationship with a young woman he had met in 1940 while he was a student at UCLA. When he met Rachel Annetta Isum, she was a freshman nursing student. A friend had introduced her to him, and

Robinson soon fell in love. At the time, he was a senior and an athletic hero to his UCLA teammates. Isum was attracted to his warm personality and confidence, but she was also taken aback by certain aspects of his personality. In fact, she said she sometimes saw him as cocky, conceited, and self-centered.

Rachel's positive feelings eventually won out, and the pair began dating. After the army drafted Robinson, he asked Rachel to marry him. She agreed, but she said she wanted to first finish her nursing studies at UCLA. She received her nursing degree in 1945.

Robinson wrote to his bride-to-be every chance he had, and he sent her chocolates every Friday. The separation was long and trying. In later years, they both looked back on this time as preparation for the struggles they would face later in their life together. Robinson often credited Rachel and his mother with being two of the most important inspirations behind everything he had attempted to do. "She [Rachel] was the guiding light behind whatever success I've had,"[1] he stated in a 1971 interview after receiving *Sport* magazine's Outstanding Athlete of the Quarter-Century Award.

Jackie Robinson and Rachel Isum were married on Feb. 10, 1946. They would have three children together—Jack, Jr., Sharon, and David.

Chapter 3: The Negro Leagues

In the year following his military discharge but before his marriage, Robinson made an important decision. He wanted to have a career in sports. In December 1945, he accepted a job as the basketball coach at Sam Houston College, a small school in Austin, Texas, which later became part of Houston-Tillotson College. Sam Houston College was an all-black school with only 35 male students.

Robinson enjoyed the opportunity to share what he had learned with the young students. He taught the team how to play fast and aggressively. As coach, he led the team to a successful season. He enjoyed the chance to be involved again in the world of sports. The money he earned, however, was barely enough to support himself. What would he do once he got married and had a family? He resigned his coaching job for a new position. His destiny would lie in the Negro leagues.

THE UNWRITTEN RULE

The Negro leagues were a collection of baseball leagues exclusively for African American and dark-skinned Hispanic players. The creation of the leagues was the result of an "unwritten rule" in which such ballplayers were barred from playing on the same teams as whites.

Organized baseball was first played in the eastern United States in the mid-1800's. By the late 1800's, people throughout the country were playing the game. In the early days of the game, amateur baseball clubs had a mix of white and black players. But the late 1800's were a time when racial discrimination was common. As baseball became more organized and professional, its development came to reflect society's discriminatory attitudes.

At the end of the 1867 season, the National Association of Baseball Players, which set the rules for amateur baseball clubs, voted to exclude from its ranks any club that had a black player on its roster. In 1869, the Cincinnati (Ohio) Red Stockings fielded a team in which all of the players were paid to play. This is why this team is considered to be the first professional baseball club. Although the Red Stockings were not bound by the rules of the National Association of Baseball Players, all of the players on the team were white.

The Red Stockings (who would later change their name to the Cincinnati Reds) helped baseball increase in popularity. One of the team's biggest fans was a young boy from Ohio named Branch Rickey, who would grow up to become general manager of the Brooklyn Dodgers team and, along with Robinson, to make baseball history.

Other professional teams soon followed in the footsteps of the Red Stockings by paying their players. In 1876, eight professional teams formed the National League, the first major league. Eight other teams formed the American League in 1900. The American League, with its status recognized in an agreement with the National League, became the second major league in 1901.

While these professional teams were forming, however, divisive racial issues began to surface in the sport. In 1884, Moses Fleetwood "Fleet" Walker, an African American player, was a catcher for the Toledo (Ohio) Blue Stockings of the Northwestern League when the Blue Stockings were admitted into the American Association, a major league organization formed in 1882 that lasted until 1891. Walker is therefore considered the first black man to play professional major league baseball. In 1887, Walker joined the Newark Little Giants of the International League. That team had another black player, a pitcher named George Stovey.

In July 1887, Cap Anson, who was the manager of the Chicago White Stockings (which became widely known as the Chicago Cubs in 1902) refused to let his team play an exhibition game against Newark unless Stovey and Walker were barred from the game. Anson's action led other ballclubs to demand that blacks be prohibited from playing alongside white players. The white team

Moses Fleetwood "Fleet" Walker became the first African American to play major league baseball in 1884, a few years before baseball erected its unofficial "color barrier."

owners banded together and agreed not to offer any major league contract to a black player. There was no official rule, but this unwritten rule was well known and strictly adhered to until 1947.

LEAGUES OF THEIR OWN

If black players wanted to play professional baseball, they would have to create leagues of their own. In the meantime, black players would organize their own individual teams and challenge one another to games. The first black professional team, created in 1885, was called the Cuban Giants. For the next 35 years, black teams would organize and disband in cities all across the United States. It was a very confusing way to run and follow the sport, but it lasted this way until the 1920's.

Black baseball remained popular, especially in cities that had large African American populations. In 1920, Rube Foster, an African American player, founded the first successful black baseball league. It was called the Negro National League.

Foster, often called the "father of black baseball," had been a pitcher for several black teams, including the Chicago Union Giants, the Cuban X-Giants of New York, the Philadelphia Giants, and the Chicago Leland Giants. In 1910, he organized a new Leland Giants team, which he renamed the American Giants the following year.

The white team owners banded together and agreed not to offer any major league contract to a black player. There was no official rule, but this unwritten rule was well known and strictly adhered to.

Foster also entered into an agreement with John Schorling, who was the brother-in-law of Charles Comiskey, owner of the major league Chicago White Sox team, and arranged for the American Giants to play their games in the White Sox's South Side Park. The White Sox left this ballpark when they moved to the newly built Comiskey Park in July 1910. The American Giants, under Foster's ownership and management until 1926, became one of the most famous black-rostered clubs in baseball history.

After becoming a baseball executive with the Negro National League, Foster would occasionally play the field and act as the team manager. He is credited with creating for black players an arena in which they could hone their talents and taste celebrity. James A. Riley, a noted author of Negro league history, called Foster "black baseball's greatest manager, the man most responsible for black baseball's continued existence, and a man almost bigger than life itself."[1]

In the footsteps of Foster's Negro National League came the formation of a second league, called the Eastern Colored League, which was formed in 1923. It lasted only five years. A replacement, the American Negro League, fared even worse, lasting only one season. Other leagues included the East-West League, Negro Southern League, and the Negro American League.

Negro league baseball featured some of the greatest players ever to pick up a baseball, including James "Cool Papa" Bell, Roy Campanella, Leon Day, Larry Doby, Josh Gibson, Monte Irwin, Walter "Buck" Leonard, and Satchel Paige. However, because of the color of their skin, most Negro league players would never be allowed to play major league baseball.

Most of these players wanted to play in the major leagues. For some of them, however, just the chance to play baseball was good enough. Throughout the history of the Negro leagues, activists and fans would point out how unfair the situation was. The players themselves did not want to dwell on this issue, however—they just wanted to play the game.

Buck Leonard, a Negro league player who would later be elected to the National Baseball Hall of Fame, which honors individuals who have made significant contributions to baseball, explained the outlook of many Negro league ball players in a 1994 book on the history of the leagues. Leonard wrote,

> I remember we played up to Griffith Stadium one Sunday and a group of black protesters was there. And they came in the clubhouse and said they wanted to talk. They said, "Don't you fellas think you could play in the major leagues?" We said, "Yeah, we think so." They said, "Would you fellas like to play in the major leagues?" "Yeah, we like to play in the major leagues," we said. "So why don't you protest or demonstrate?" they said. We said, "You fellas

demonstrate and protest, we gonna play. We don't have time." They said, "Well, aren't you part of the movement?" We said, "We're part of the game, not the movement. We're part of baseball."[2]

In time, younger Negro league ballplayers would become part of a "movement" to the major leagues. Players like Hank Aaron, Ernie Banks, and Willie Mays, who started in the Negro leagues, would all go on to become superstars in the major leagues. But Jackie Robinson would arrive there first.

THE KANSAS CITY MONARCHS

In 1945, Robinson joined the Kansas City (Missouri) Monarchs. The Monarchs team was one of the best-known and most successful of all the Negro league teams. Robinson met one of its players, who told him that the Monarchs were looking for talented additions to the club. Robinson wrote a letter to the owner of the team, who looked into his background. Impressed by what he had discovered, the owner invited Robinson to join the team as its new shortstop. He offered Robinson $400 (about $4,325 today) a month. Robinson considered the paycheck to be "a financial bonanza."[3]

Robinson was 26 years old, and he had to prove himself to the other players on the team. Some of these men had been playing in the Negro leagues for almost as long as Robinson had been alive. Furthermore, some of the players resented Robinson because he had gone to college and had also achieved some level of success on the playing field. Although he had played

Rube Foster, the "father of black baseball," founded the first successful African American baseball league in 1920.

college baseball and semiprofessional football, Robinson had no experience when it came to professional baseball. For a while, Robinson wondered whether he had made a mistake in pursuing a baseball career.

One famous Negro league player was Jimmie Crutchfield. He was playing for the Chicago American Giants in 1945 when the team faced the Kansas City Monarchs and Robinson in an exhibition game. Crutchfield was a veteran player who freely admitted that he was not impressed by Robinson at first glance. "I remember seeing Jackie for the first time. He was fat. And I thought the Monarchs had him just for a publicity stunt because he had been so great in college,"[4] he said. But Crutchfield learned to admire Robinson after watching him play.

For his part, the college-educated Robinson was a bit surprised by the conditions endured by his teammates. For many of them, it was the only life they had ever known but, for Jackie Robinson, it was an eye-opening experience.

The Monarchs, like all Negro league teams, would crisscross the United States to challenge other teams. Long bus trips could be followed by a *double-header* (two baseball games between the same teams played one after the other on the same day) and then a return bus trip. Finding a place to eat was often difficult, because many establishments would not serve African American clients. Sometimes, a restaurant owner would allow a team to purchase food but not eat it inside. The black players had to take the food and eat it on the bus as they left town. The players would often be forced to sleep on the bus or outside at the playing field if the town they were visiting did not have a hotel that accepted African Americans.

White ballplayers did not face such dilemmas, why should black ballplayers? Robinson often wondered this, but there was no easy answer. It was the way life was in the United States at that time. Even so, Robinson wondered if there would ever be a time when blacks would be treated fairly. He also wondered whether his time would be better spent finding ways to eliminate racial discrimination. Many times he felt trapped. His teammates did not

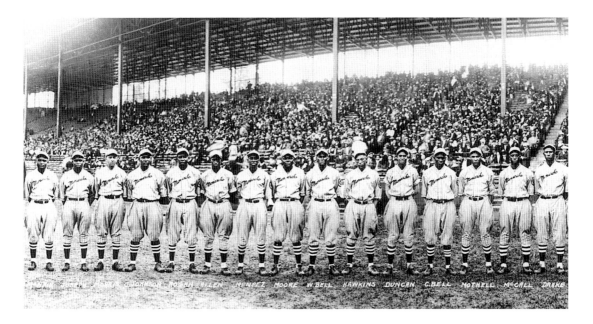

always like him. Most of the other players had played together for years, and some of them resented this "rookie" Negro leaguer with his college education.

Robinson did not like the situation in which he had placed himself, and he sometimes criticized the living and playing conditions. But then his teammates made it clear that they did not care to hear his complaints, either. Robinson was left to wonder: Had he made a terrible mistake by pursuing a career in baseball?

The Kansas City Monarchs were one of the most popular African American baseball teams. This photo shows a Monarchs team in 1924.

NATURAL ABILITY

Robinson's natural ability, however, began to shine through as soon as he stepped onto the playing field. When he was on the field, some of his doubts, at least temporarily, faded away. Many of the younger Monarchs players were away, still finishing their tours of duty in the armed services at the end of World War II. Because of his talent, Robinson was able to help fill the gap they left. He proved to be a powerful hitter for the Monarchs, with a *batting average* of about .345. (Batting average shows the percentage of times that a player gets a base hit. It is the number of hits divided by the number of official times that the player has been at bat.) He also was an aggressive base stealer and base runner. His winning attitude helped bolster the team and encourage other players to play harder.

In his first year in the Negro leagues, Jackie Robinson was well on his way to establishing himself as a star player. His style of play earned him a spot on the Negro National League All-Star team. Although shortstop was not his best position, the coaches and manager of the Monarchs had faith in his ability and planned on working with him so that, upon his return to the Monarchs from the All-Star team, he would be better.

Little did anyone know that Jackie Robinson's first season in the Negro leagues would also be his last.

Chapter 4: The Noble Experiment

Branch Rickey was born in Ohio in 1881 and had played some major league baseball. In 1904, he was the baseball coach at Ohio Wesleyan University (OWU) in Delaware, Ohio. During a road trip to South Bend, Indiana, the OWU team had reservations at a local hotel. When Rickey and the team entered the lobby, the hotel clerk was surprised to see a black player, whose name was Charles Thomas, traveling with the team. The clerk informed Rickey that the hotel allowed only white guests and Thomas could not stay there. Rickey was indignant and threatened to move the entire team out of the hotel.

Fortunately for the team, Rickey was also a persuasive man. After meeting privately with the manager, the hotel agreed to let Thomas share a room with Rickey. Thomas, however, was hurt by the experience.

Years later, Rickey described how later in the hotel room he saw Thomas fighting tears and rubbing his hands, lamenting the color of his own skin. The experience made Rickey realize the kind of deep pain that racial segregation could cause. The OWU coach promised to always do whatever he could to see that other African Americans did not have to face the bitter humiliation that his friend faced because of racism.[1]

Branch Rickey saw his African American teammate Charles Thomas fighting tears and rubbing his hands, lamenting the color of his own skin. The experience made Rickey realize the kind of deep pain that racial segregation could cause.

Rickey would spend more than two decades working as an executive within the St. Louis Cardinals organization. While there, he tried to eliminate the seating arrangement in which black fans had to sit in a section removed from white spectators at Sportsmen's Park, the stadium in which the Cardinals played ball. He was unsuccessful in this effort, but Rickey was not about to give up his fight.

In 1942, Rickey accepted a job as president of the Brooklyn

Dodgers in New York. Once again, racial segregation weighed heavily on his mind. The time had come to integrate baseball. Rickey persuaded the team owners to allow him to explore the possibility of adding an African American player to their roster.

Historians have long speculated about the exact reason Rickey wanted to integrate baseball. Some believe that Rickey was trying to make amends for what had happened to Charles Thomas when he was a college coach. Others say that by opening up the playing field to talented African American players, Rickey hoped to improve the Dodgers' chances for winning a National League championship—or even the *World Series* (the major league baseball championship of the United States). The Dodgers were in need of talented new players when Rickey took over as general manager. There are other opinions as well, including one that maintains that Rickey envisioned a place for himself in history if his plan worked.

> *"If a black boy can make it on Okinawa and Guadalcanal, hell, he can make it in baseball."*
>
> Baseball commissioner
> A. B. "Happy" Chandler, 1944

No matter what his motivation was, Rickey was well aware that his plan would not be easily accepted. The commissioner of baseball (the administrative head of major league baseball), Kenesaw Mountain Landis, was firmly behind baseball's unwritten rule that barred blacks from the game. Publicly, Landis steadfastly denied there was a color barrier—official or unofficial—in organized baseball. Most baseball historians, however, considered Landis to be a major obstacle to baseball's *integration* (the inclusion of all people on an equal basis).

Rickey knew that if Landis learned of his plan, the commissioner would not be pleased. Similarly, fans, players, and other team owners would likely resent the idea and try to force him to abandon it. Things might even turn violent. However, a change was needed in baseball, and someone had to have the courage to begin the process.

On Nov. 25, 1944, Landis died. The new baseball commissioner, A. B. "Happy" Chandler, did not share his predecessor's viewpoint about racial segregation. Chandler was a former governor of Kentucky and a former U.S. senator. One day, he was asked what he thought about the prospect of an African American playing in the big leagues. With the United States involved in World War II and black soldiers and sailors dying to defend the country, Chandler decided to take a stand that was much different from the one Landis had long held. "If a black boy can make it on Okinawa and Guadalcanal [sites of two fierce battles during the war], hell, he can make it in baseball," Chandler said. He also stated, "I don't believe in barring Negroes from baseball just because they are Negroes."[2]

Baseball commissioner A. B. "Happy" Chandler, right, took a stand against segregation in the major leagues that gave Branch Rickey the impetus to move forward with his plan to add an African American to the Dodgers. Chandler is shown speaking with National League President Ford Frick before a World Series game in Chicago in 1945.

Chandler's comment alone did not eliminate racial segregation in the major leagues, but it did give Rickey the impetus to move forward with his plan to add an African American player to the Dodgers.

This new ballplayer would come from the Negro leagues. Although Rickey also sent *scouts* (people who gather information about athletes or athletic teams) to Latin American and Caribbean countries to identify promising dark-skinned players, he knew that the Negro leagues had many promising athletes who were prevented from playing in the majors because of the color of their skin. He decided it was in the Negro leagues that the future of integrated baseball would be found. However, the man to break the color barrier would have to embody a perfect mixture of athleticism, dignity, and the tolerance of an expected racial backlash. Did a player like this exist?

FINDING THE RIGHT PLAYER

Another challenging part of Rickey's idea was persuading baseball scouts to analyze the various players without revealing the true nature of his plan. In 1943, Rickey concocted a cover story about plans to start a new Negro league team. He used the cover to send scouts out in search of talented, young black players.

Rickey studied the scouting reports and considered several players for the honor of being the first black player in the modern major leagues. There were many big-name players who would have drawn attention to his plan had they been chosen. Among the Negro league players considered were pitcher Satchel Paige and catcher Roy Campanella. Although neither was chosen by Rickey as the big leagues' first black player, both men would eventually find their way to the major leagues. Paige would become the major leagues' first black pitcher, and Campanella would become the major leagues' first black catcher.

For nearly two years, Rickey was able to keep his plan a secret from everyone but his most trusted confidantes. Meanwhile, some political activists and members of the black press were increasingly pressuring the major league owners to allow black players to try out for the teams.

In the spring of 1945, Rickey announced that he planned to create a new team called the Brooklyn Brown Dodgers to play in a newly formed Negro league called the United States League. This new league existed briefly, for only one season. It was primarily meant as a ruse to conceal Rickey's still-developing operation to integrate baseball.

The trick bought Rickey more time. Now he could openly send out his top scouts, supposedly to fill the ranks of the Brown Dodgers. Several reports crossed Rickey's desk that he found intriguing. One report in particular informed the Dodgers general manager about a player who seemed to match Rickey's criteria. That player was Jackie Robinson.

Rickey sent a scout named Clyde Sukeforth to tell Robinson that the Dodgers general manager wanted to meet with him in

New York City. It was not an uncommon practice for Negro league players to jump from one team to another in search of more money. Still, the idea of meeting with another team made Robinson nervous. What if the Monarchs fired him for speaking with another owner? Sukeforth told Robinson that if that happened, there was nothing he could do, but meeting with Rickey was extremely important.

THE HISTORIC MEETING

On Aug. 28, 1945, Rickey and Robinson sat down for what would be a historic encounter. Rickey knew all about Robinson's extraordinary athletic ability. He knew that Robinson had played alongside black and white players in college. After meeting with Robinson, Rickey also learned that Robinson was strongly committed to his family and that Robinson's deep religious convictions were reflective of his own strong religious beliefs. Robinson told Rickey that he neither smoked nor drank, but that he was a fiery competitor on the playing field.

Both Rickey and Robinson were cautious with one another at first. Rickey wanted to know more about Robinson's family life, for example. But Rickey then disclosed his real plan to Robinson. He told Robinson that life as the first modern-era major league black ballplayer would be difficult for him and his family. There would be opposition to his playing. Most notably, Rickey warned Robinson that he would have to accept all of the expected verbal abuse without fighting back. The role of not fighting back was one that Robinson was not accustomed to playing.

To demonstrate his point, Rickey launched into a racist tirade, acting out the role of a racist fan and then the role of a racist teammate. (Robinson would encounter both during his playing career.) Rickey explained that this would be the kind of abuse Robinson could expect as a black player in the white major leagues, and that he was testing Robinson's reaction to such abuse. Rickey added that pitchers would deliberately throw at Robinson to try to hit him, and runners would slide into him. He kept hammering home his point—it would not be an easy time for Robinson.

The inflammatory words and harsh scenarios angered Robinson, but he managed to keep his composure. He sat there and listened to Rickey's description of the harsh reality of what was to come if he accepted the general manager's offer—and he restrained himself from fighting back.

Years after their conversation, Robinson recalled some of what had taken place. He said that Rickey had told him, "We can't fight our way through this, Robinson. We've got no army. There's virtually nobody on our side. No owners, no umpires, very few newspapermen. And I'm afraid that many fans will be hostile. We'll be in a tough position. We can win only if we can convince the world that I'm doing this because you're a great ballplayer and a fine gentleman."

Then Rickey asked, "Have you got the guts to play the game no matter what happens?"

"I think I can play the game, Mr. Rickey," replied Robinson, but his anger still boiled within him. During years of facing segregation and discrimination—as a child, in school, in the army—Robinson had always believed in standing up against hate and unfairness. What followed was one of the most famous exchanges in baseball history.

He asked, "Mr. Rickey, are you looking for a Negro who is afraid to fight back?"

Rickey replied, "Robinson, I'm looking for a ballplayer with guts enough not to fight back."[3]

Robinson thought for a moment. His daughter, Sharon Robinson, would later write that her father viewed the offer as more than just an opportunity to play baseball. Here was a chance "to avenge the racism of his boyhood, to help right injustice."[4]

Robinson and Rickey spoke further about the importance of Robinson's role in major league baseball should he agree to break baseball's color barrier, including the responsibilities it would mean for himself and the opportunities it would mean for other African American ballplayers.

ROBINSON'S NEW JOURNEY

To assist Robinson on his new journey in life, Rickey established a list of "do's and don't's" that Robinson was to follow upon accepting the offer. For example, Robinson could not make *product endorsements* (be paid to promote or advertise a product) during most of his first season. Nor could he have his name listed as the author of a newspaper or magazine article. These rules were established because Rickey did not want his plans with Robinson to be viewed as a publicity stunt or political statement.

Most importantly, if Robinson got a bad call (a call he disagreed with or that he believed was incorrect) from an umpire, he could not object. And if another player insulted him, he had to ignore the insult. For his own protection, Robinson was required to leave various stadiums (including the Dodgers' stadium) by exits separate from those used by the rest of the team. He was also told to stay out of the public eye when he was not playing ball.

"Robinson, I'm looking for a ballplayer with guts enough not to fight back."

Branch Rickey to Jackie Robinson, Aug. 28, 1945

What has become known as "The Noble Experiment" had begun.

At the end of their three-hour meeting, only one more detail needed to be addressed. Rickey insisted that Robinson pledge not to tell anyone (besides his closest family members) about what they had discussed. Once again, Robinson agreed to do as he had been asked.

For nearly two months, Robinson kept his promise to Rickey. In October 1945, Robinson received word that he was to travel to Montreal, Canada, to sign a contract with the Montreal Royals, the minor league affiliate of the Brooklyn Dodgers. (Rickey believed that racial pressures during Robinson's first year would be less intense in Canada.) Under the terms of his contract, Robinson was paid $600 (about $6,500 today) a month salary and received a $3,500 (about $37,850 today) signing bonus. On Oct. 23, 1945, the Dodgers formally announced that they had signed Jackie Robinson.

Robinson discusses his contract for the 1950 season with Brooklyn Dodgers general manager Branch Rickey, the man who signed him to the team in 1947.

Rickey was right to have predicted an uproar. A 1947 *Time* magazine article recalled,

> . . . when Rickey hired Jackie away from the Monarchs there were loud and angry outcries, and not all of them were in a Southern accent. Some of the ugliest comments were spoken in ripe, raucous Brooklynese. Even some owners in the low-paying Negro leagues protested against "raiding" their men . . . Jackie faced hostility, suspicion, curiosity and every newspaper camera within miles when he reported to the International League's Montreal club for training.[5]

The Kansas City Monarchs considered suing Robinson and the Brooklyn Dodgers for breach of contract. Some major league owners privately supported the Monarchs, hoping to keep the color barrier intact. In addition, because many owners profited by renting their ballparks to Negro league teams, they did not want those teams to start losing players and money. But when African American sports writers and fans swung their support behind Robinson, the Monarchs withdrew their threatened lawsuit.

Before heading to Canada, Robinson accompanied a black All-Star team to Venezuela. While there, he began to wonder what he had gotten himself into. Perhaps he was not the right man for the job. After joining the Montreal Royals in 1946, he proved everyone—including himself—wrong.

He was the first black player in the International League in 57 years, but that fact did not intimidate Robinson. In his first game, he hit a home run and three singles. He also stole two bases. Robinson batted .349 for the Royals during the 1946 season. He also scored 113 runs, ranked second in the International League in stolen bases, and won the league's Most Valuable Player award. He was the main reason the Royals won the *pennant* (championship) in their division that year—with a remarkable 19 ½-game lead—as well as the Little World Series (the minor league championship).

At the end of the 1946 season, Robinson returned to his home in California. In the spring of 1947, Robinson reported for training in Canada with the Montreal Royals. Yet another baseball season was set to begin, and he was still in the minor leagues. Robinson had faith, though, that Branch Rickey knew what he was doing. After all, it was Rickey's master plan that had taken Robinson this far, and he was not about to lose faith now.

Chapter 5: Breaking the Color Barrier

In anticipation of a game between the Royals and the Dodgers, Rickey told Robinson,

> *I want you to be a whirling demon against the Dodgers. I want you to concentrate, to hit that ball, to get on base by any means necessary. I want you to run wild, to steal the pants off them, to be the most conspicuous player on the field—but conspicuous only because of the kind of baseball you're playing. Not only will you impress the Dodger players, but the stories that the newspapermen send back to Brooklyn and New York newspapers will help create demand on the part of the fans that you be brought up to the majors.*[1]

Robinson's chance to display his talent came in March and April 1947, when the Royals faced the Dodgers in a number of exhibition games. Robinson batted .625 during the Dodgers-Royals match-ups. He also stole seven bases. Even so, neither the Dodgers organization nor the team's fans cried out for the addition of Robinson. Rickey had hoped that attention from Dodger fans would compel the organization to sign Robinson.

Rickey came up with another idea. Early in *spring training* (the time during which players practice in a warm climate after the baseball season winter break), Rickey had Robinson start playing as first baseman—a position in which the Dodgers were weak. He planned to have the Dodgers manager, Leo Durocher, claim that the team needed fresh talent at first base and Robinson was the best prospect. Durocher had already done his part in averting a potential disaster during spring training when he learned that some of his players were circulating a petition to block Robinson from joining the team. Durocher, who was never at a loss for words, suggested that his players immediately stop the petition or he would stop it for them. The players complied.

Before Rickey could enact his plan involving Durocher, the manager was suspended for the season for conduct harmful to baseball, including allegedly associating with known gamblers. Rickey could wait no longer. On April 10, 1947, he sent a note to the press box during a Dodgers-Royals exhibition game mentioning that the Brooklyn Dodgers had just purchased Jackie Robinson's contract from the Montreal Royals. It was official: baseball's long-standing color barrier had been broken. The major leagues were about to be integrated, and Jackie Robinson was the man who was going to do it. The following day, Robinson played an exhibition game as a member of the Dodgers.

On April 15, 1947, Robinson wore the Brooklyn Dodgers' blue as he took to the field in the opening game of the team's regular season. His uniform number was 42. Although Robinson failed to get a hit, the Dodgers won 5-3 over the Boston Braves.

After joining the Dodgers, Robinson's playing deteriorated for a period. He had a great deal of trouble hitting the ball. Many of the fans who came to Ebbets Field to see him play were

Robinson poses with his Dodgers teammates on the steps of the dugout during his first game with the team on April 15, 1947. From left to right are Johnny "Spider" Jorgensen, Harold "Pee Wee" Reese, Eddie Stanky, and Robinson.

Dodgers shortstop "Pee Wee" Reese tosses the ball to second baseman Robinson during a spring training game in Florida in 1950.

disappointed. Those who had been against the addition of Robinson to the team felt that they were being proved right. Adding to the pressure, Robinson was dealing with racist taunts from the crowds, both at home and on the road. It's possible that this pressure contributed to the temporary slump in Robinson's playing.

Things were going to get worse before they got better. Robinson and his family began receiving hate mail. Some of it arrived at Ebbets Field. Some of it was sent directly to his home. Some of the letters were threatening. The writers said they would kill Robinson and his wife or kidnap their infant son, Jack Jr.

Another problem was that some cities in which the Dodgers played were heavily segregated. In Philadelphia, while in town to play the Phillies, Robinson was denied entry into the team's hotel.

A person who could have been one of Robinson's greatest enemies turned out to be one of his greatest friends. He was the Dodgers captain, Harold "Pee Wee" Reese. Reese had been born in Kentucky, and many people thought a Southerner like Reese would have a problem with a black teammate. To complicate matters, Reese was the Dodgers' shortstop, a position that Robinson played on the Monarchs. What would happen if Robinson took Reese's position?

In the spring of 1947, Reese told journalists that he was willing to give Robinson a chance to prove himself as a player. Reese also admitted that he did not think he would be able to stand up to the kind of scrutiny that Robinson had endured since joining the team. In one away game during the season, the heckling became almost unbearable for Robinson. Reese could tell that the latest addition to the Dodgers' family was at a breaking point. Furthermore, opposing players began shouting taunts at Reese, asking how a white man from Kentucky could play alongside an African American player.

Because of his agreement with Rickey, there was nothing Robinson could do but stand there and take the verbal abuse. Reese, however, had made no such promise to Rickey. As team captain, Reese realized he had to set a tone for the team. So, one day he sent a clear message to baseball fans as to what he thought about playing with Robinson. Reese refused to respond to the hecklers or even look in their direction. Instead, he walked over, put his arm around Robinson's shoulder, and engaged him in conversation.

Neither man would later remember what was said that day. It did not really matter what the words were, anyway. The heckling stopped, and that moment sparked the beginning of a solid friendship that would last 25 years. When Robinson switched to playing second base in 1948, he and Reese also became a powerful infield combination.

As Robinson gained greater acceptance from the Dodgers, he slowly came out of his slump and began producing runs for the team. He also began to use his impressive speed and to show off his intelligence and daring at stealing bases. His fellow Dodgers enjoyed these performances, as did the fans. Although the hate mail never stopped, Robinson also began receiving letters of encouragement—from people who were both fans and nonfans and both black and white.

Baseball attendance by African American fans grew significantly in 1947. They all wanted to see Jackie Robinson take the field. The Dodgers franchise earned about $150,000 ($1,300,000 today) in extra ticket sales in 1947, thanks to the presence of their new infielder. The increase in the number of fans took place not only in Brooklyn, but in nearly every National League park that the Dodgers visited that year. Baseball attendance in the National League increased by more than 750,000 people in 1947 over attendance during the previous season. The increase helped the

Dodgers set a club attendance record in 1947, with more than 1.8 million fans passing through the turnstiles.

The majority of Robinson's teammates, however, remained unsure how to interact with him off the field. At first, most of them chose not to interact at all. Many times, Robinson would sit alone in the clubhouse or during the trip to another city. Sometimes he would talk with Reese or the black journalists who were traveling with the team, but for the most part he wrote letters to his wife or to friends back in California. In one letter, Robinson expressed compassion for those who did not know how to act around him. He said that he had been on teams with white players before, but this was the first time his teammates shared their locker room—a traditional place of team camaraderie—with a black man.

TURNING THE OTHER CHEEK

By June 1947, Robinson and his teammates had grown more comfortable around each other. During train trips to games, some of the other players would invite him to join in their conversations or card games. He was now part of the team, both on and off the field.

Players on other teams were less considerate. During a series of Dodgers home games in April, the manager of the Philadelphia Phillies, a man named Ben Chapman, had openly supported his team's verbal abuse of Robinson. To his credit, Robinson ignored the comments, and the owners of the Phillies eventually sent a message to Chapman instructing him and his team to stop their cruel taunts.

In May, when the Dodgers made their first trip of the season to St. Louis, newspapers reported rumors that some Cardinals players might strike if Robinson played. The National League president, Ford Frick, threatened to suspend any player who took such action. No player did.

During many games, pitchers on opposing teams tried to hit Robinson with the ball, and runners slid into him with their sharp cleats. Rickey had not exaggerated when he said that life in the majors would be brutal for Robinson. Through it all, however,

Robinson did not lash out at any of these players. The rest of the Dodgers began to defend Robinson on the field and retaliate when other team's players tried to harm him, either physically or verbally.

During the 1947 season, Robinson saw action in 151 of the 154 regular season games, more than any other Dodger that season. As the team's first baseman, he brought an aggressive style to the game. He finished first in the National League in stolen bases and second in runs scored. In addition, he led the team in singles, bunt hits, and total bases.

As Branch Rickey had hoped, Jackie Robinson did help to turn around the team's misfortunes of the past decades. In 1947, the team won the National League pennant and went on to face the New York Yankees in the World Series. The Dodgers lost a close series in seven games. Robinson would be back the following season.

In September 1947, the growing number of Jackie Robinson supporters staged "Jackie Robinson Day" at Ebbets Field to honor their newfound hero. Fans presented him with a number of gifts, including a new car and watch. Jack Semel, a Dodgers season ticket holder, also presented him with a plaque to commemorate the beginning of interracial goodwill in major league baseball.

Subjected to reprehensible abuse by fans and opponents during the 1947 season, Robinson conducted himself in an irreproachable way. In recognition of his impressive season, *The Sporting News* (baseball's trade newspaper) and the Baseball Writers' Association named him the first-ever National League *Rookie* (first-season player) of the Year.

In its report on the award, *The Sporting News* noted,

That Jackie Roosevelt Robinson might have had more obstacles than his first-year competitors, and that he perhaps had a harder fight to gain even major league recognition, was no concern of this publication. The sociological experiment that Robinson represented, the trail-blazing that he did, the barriers he broke down, did not enter into the decision. He was rated and examined solely as a freshman player in the big leagues—on the basis of his hitting, his running, his defensive play, his team value.[2]

TIME
THE WEEKLY NEWSMAGAZINE

JACKIE ROBINSON
He and the boys took a chance.
[*sport*]

Robinson made the cover of Time *magazine, Sept. 22, 1947, when he was honored as the National League's Rookie of the Year.*

Ironically, *The Sporting News* had also published an article early in the season proclaiming that it would be impossible for a black man to succeed in the major leagues.

At the end of the season, Robinson and black sportswriter Wendell Smith began to write a book about his life. *Jackie Robinson: My Own Story* was published in 1948. A public opinion poll listed him as the second most popular person in America in 1947 that year. Only American singer and movie actor Bing Crosby ranked higher.

Following Robinson's Rookie of the Year selection, various publications shone the spotlight on him, his family, and his background. In a cover story in the Sept. 22, 1947, issue of *Time*, the magazine recounted some of Robinson's early experiences on the field:

It was only a month since Speedster Enos Slaughter of the St. Louis Cardinals, galloping into first base, had spiked First Baseman Jackie Robinson. Jackie, the first avowed Negro in the history of big-league baseball, looked at his ripped stocking and bleeding leg. It might have been an accident, but Jackie didn't think so. Neither did a lot of others who saw the play. Jackie set his teeth, and said nothing. He didn't dare to.

Last week, the Brooklyn Dodgers faced the Cards again, and this time the pennant—and the Dodgers' none-too-healthy 4 ½-game lead—was at stake. The Cards, somewhat housebroken descendants of the rough-&-tumble Gashouse Gang, were fighting back, late and hard. In the second inning, Jackie Robinson was spiked again—this time by trigger-tempered Catcher Joe Garagiola.

Next inning, at the plate, there was a face-to-face exchange of hot words between Robinson and Garagiola—the kind of rough passage that fans appreciatively call a "rhubarb." Umpire "Beans" Reardon hastily stepped between the two and broke it up. That was the end of it: no fisticuffs on the field, no rioting in the stands. But it was a sign, and an important one, that Jackie had established himself as a big leaguer. He had earned what comes free to every other player; the right to squawk.[3]

In reality, this type of outburst was a rare occurrence. It would be another year until Robinson was entirely able to speak his mind as a ballplayer.

In 1948, Robinson reported overweight to spring training, and an unhappy manager Durocher (who had returned from his suspension) took notice. Durocher blasted Robinson and made him work hard—in front of his teammates and the press—to get back into shape. This time, the shouting was not because of the color of his skin. The team had begun to accept Robinson as "another ballplayer" and Durocher was treating him like one.

So were the umpires. During a game against the Pittsburgh Pirates that season, Robinson was ejected from a game for heckling an umpire. Race had nothing to do with it. It was all just part of the game. Robinson was "just one of the guys." The tide was turning; Robinson was on his own as a ballplayer.

Robinson argues with umpire Al Barlick, after Barlick called him out at second base, in a game against the New York Giants on Sept. 6, 1952.

Chapter 6: Integrating the Major Leagues

Robinson no longer had to shoulder the burden of being the only African American player in the major leagues. On July 5, 1947, Bill Veeck, owner of the Cleveland (Ohio) Indians of the American League, signed Larry Doby, a star player with the Newark Eagles. Doby became the first African American in the American League.

As had been the case with Rickey and Robinson, Veeck gave Doby a list of tips on how to act on and off the field. The American League suggestions were similar to the "rules" prescribed by Rickey to Robinson for the National League. Doby knew, as did Robinson, that if integration of major league baseball was to continue, the guidelines would have to be met. The two men would often call each other to gain strength from their shared burden.

Robinson and Doby were followed into the big leagues in 1947 by African American players Hank Thompson and Willard Brown, who both joined the St. Louis Browns in late July. In August, the Dodgers added an African American player named Dan Bankhead to their roster. Thompson and Brown did not perform well and lasted for only a few weeks on the Browns. Thompson returned to the big leagues during the 1949 season and played several years with the New York Giants. Meanwhile, Bankhead pitched the rest of the 1947 season.

By the late 1940's, some progress in integration was being made on teams throughout the majors, but slowly. On July 7, 1948, Veeck signed legendary Negro league pitcher Satchel Paige to play for the Cleveland Indians. At age 42, Paige became the "oldest rookie" in the major leagues. Roy Campanella joined the Dodgers in 1948, followed by Don Newcombe in 1949. However, by 1951, only 5 of the 16 major league teams had been integrated. In September 1953, there were black players on 6 of the 16 teams. It was not until 1959, when the Boston Red Sox called up Pumpsie Green from the minor leagues, that every major league club had a black player on its roster.

If Robinson's freshman year in the majors was groundbreaking, his sophomore season could best be described as lackluster. Even Robinson admitted that after starting the season in a slump, the only highlights of the year were being moved to second base and being tossed out of a game by an umpire.

Things improved the following year. In 1949, Robinson was voted to play in his first All-Star Game. That same year, Robinson won the National League batting title and the league's Most Valuable Player award. He led the majors with 37 stolen bases, which was the highest National League total since 1930. He also hit .342 and knocked in 124 runs.

In addition, 1949 was the year that Rickey told Robinson he was on his own—that is, he no longer had to abide by the list of "do's and don't's" that had been established for him. Robinson also signed a new contract for the 1950 season, earning $35,000 (about $283,000 today) a year.

The year 1950 not only marked the start of a new decade, but also major changes for the Dodgers organization— and for Robinson personally. At the end of the regular season, Branch Rickey left the Dodgers to join the Pittsburgh Pirates as vice president and general manager. If Robinson thought that the prior season was one in which he was on his own, what would the coming years mean, without his mentor and friend?

Larry Doby stands in the dugout in July 1947 after being signed by Cleveland Indians owner Bill Veeck as the first African American player in the American League.

ON HIS OWN

For the next few seasons, Robinson continued to hone his skills as a baseball player. He also spoke out about the need for the continued integration of major league teams. Some fans and owners did not like it when Robinson would take on such a heated topic, but their opposition did not bother him. After all, Robinson believed that there was no one better suited to discuss the topic of racial integration than the man who had broken the color barrier. Even so, his stance often resulted in bitter arguments pitting Robinson against both the press and officials in the Dodgers organization.

In both 1952 and 1953, the Dodgers won the National League pennant and went to the World Series. Both times, they lost to the rival New York Yankees.

In 1952, when he was a guest on a television show, Robinson made a comment that resulted in an uproar from fans, mainly Yankees fans. A teen-ager asked him if he thought the Yankees were prejudiced because they did not yet have any black players. Robinson replied that while he admired the players that they did have, he thought that the team was wrong in not having any blacks on the team.

The Yankees' management did not like people—even Jackie Robinson—saying that they were against blacks in baseball. They denied the charge and said that Robinson was just trying to start trouble. Ford Frick, who was now the commissioner of baseball, met with Robinson and scolded him for his comments. Robinson would not apologize. Frick explained that he did not want an apology. In fact, he wanted Robinson to speak his mind. However, Frick also wanted Robinson to back up any accusations with facts. Following their meeting, Robinson felt as though he had found another ally in his fight against racism in baseball.

The pressure of being the first black ballplayer, fighting for equal rights for present and future African American players, and his concern over the way that the Dodgers were being managed, caused Robinson to consider leaving the sport as early as 1954. He knew he was reaching the end of his peak years as an athlete. He had caused enough trouble in the majors to guarantee that he would not be offered an administrative or coaching position. Perhaps, he thought, it was time to find something in private industry. Robinson spent the next year making calls and building contacts in preparation for a life outside of baseball.

In 1955, however, the Brooklyn Dodgers put together one of their best teams in years and once again found themselves in the World Series. And again they were facing the New York Yankees. In the first game of the 1955 World Series, Robinson recorded a memorable baseball moment when he stole home. Although the Dodgers lost that game, they would go on to win the World Series. It was the team's first World Series championship.

SETTING NEW SIGHTS

In 1956, Robinson was not playing as well as he had in the past and was spending more time on the bench and less time on the field. It took him longer to recover between games, and he experienced constant aches and pains. He was now a nine-year veteran of the Brooklyn Dodgers. The team dynasty of the 1950's was coming to a close. He knew it was time to leave the game.

As he made plans for his life after baseball, he kept his intentions a secret. He did not want anyone to know that the 1956 campaign would be his last. He had also struck a deal with the editors of *Look,* a popular American magazine of the day, in which the magazine paid him a large sum of money to be allowed to reveal that he was retiring.

For the sixth time in nine years, the 1956 World Series included the Brooklyn Dodgers. In the sixth game of the series, played against the New York Yankees, Robinson got a hit to win the game and tie the series three games to three. That would be his final hit in a major league baseball game. In game seven, Robinson was hitless. He was also the last batter, and, as a footnote to a long career, he struck out. The Yankees won the series.

In mid-December 1956, on the day before Robinson was to sign a contract for a new job following his baseball career, Dodgers management sent him a message that they wanted to meet with him.

They did not know that he was already planning to leave the team. The next day, immediately after signing the contract for his new job, Robinson phoned the Dodgers general manager. He discovered that the team had news for him—he had been traded to the New York Giants in exchange for pitcher Dick Littlefield and $30,000 (about $215,000 today).

In early January 1957, the issue of *Look* containing news of Robinson's retirement hit subscriber mailboxes and newsstands. No one could believe it. First came the news that Robinson had been traded, and now he was retiring. For many baseball fans it was a devastating blow for the game.

The Giants organization offered Robinson as much as $60,000 (about $430,000 today) a year to sign a contract with the team. Robinson briefly entertained the idea. Children—especially African American children—looked up to him and admired him. Should he stay in the game?

Then Robinson learned that the Dodgers' management was discounting the magazine article as just a ploy to try to get more money from the Giants. This was not true, and Robinson did not want people to think that it was.

The Brooklyn Dodgers celebrate on the field after defeating the New York Yankees in the seventh game of the 1955 World Series to win their first World Series championship.

In his playing career, Robinson had been named the 1947 Rookie of the Year, won an award as the 1949 National League's Most Valuable Player, and played in six All-Star Games. Furthermore, he was a batting, fielding, and stolen-base champion. He led second basemen in *double-plays* (putting out two players in one play) for four consecutive years, and he had a lifetime batting average of .311 and a total of 197 stolen bases. These all were impressive statistics, and many people wondered what type of statistics he would have posted had he played in the majors before age 28.

What fans, teammates, and competitors could no longer deny was that Jackie Robinson was a fierce competitor on the field and one of the greatest ballplayers of the 1950's. But the time had come to move on. There were new challenges to meet.

Chapter 7: A Champion Off the Field

Life without baseball was going to be very different for Jackie Robinson. Yet, he was sure he had made the right choice by leaving the sport. For better or for worse, he was a Brooklyn Dodger, and he could not see himself playing for any other team. There were times, however, when Robinson hoped that another baseball team would offer him a job as a coach or manager. No such offer was ever made, so he eventually abandoned the idea of participating in baseball again. A life outside of baseball certainly was not the first obstacle he had faced in his lifetime, and it was not going to be the last.

MINORITY BUSINESSMAN AND POLITICIAN

Shortly after deciding to retire from baseball, Robinson accepted a job as vice president and director of personnel with Chock Full O'Nuts, a New York City-based company that made a brand of coffee and owned a chain of fast-food restaurants in New York state. One of the reasons he accepted the position with Chock Full O'Nuts was that it was one of the few companies at the time with a policy of hiring large numbers of minority employees. The owner hoped that Robinson would, among other things, serve as a role model for the employees. Robinson viewed his position as a chance to further improve conditions for black workers in the United States.

His new white-collar job was more of a regular routine than his days with the Dodgers. He drove to New York City every morning from Stamford, Connecticut, and worked in his office. He also often had to drive to the company's restaurants to check on business. He enjoyed speaking with the restaurant employees, many of whom were African Americans from low-income families. Their stories of childhood and growing up were similar to Robinson's own. He used the opportunity to tell the African American workers that they should not let their poor backgrounds stop them from achieving great things. Many of these people understood and appreciated what Robinson was trying to tell them, and they admired him for it.

Robinson may no longer have been waving to tens of thousands of cheering fans at Ebbets Field, but the chance to speak one-on-one with fans and with members of his own race who were struggling, as he once had, was fulfilling in its own way. In addition, his wife and children were glad that he was home more often than when he was a member of the Dodgers.

In time, Robinson became active in politics. For several years, he had tried to distance himself from any sort of political involvement but, because his baseball career was over, he slowly became more active in civil rights and social issues.

In 1960, Robinson, like all Americans, had the opportunity to choose between two very different men who wanted to be elected president of the United States. One of these individuals was Democratic candidate John F. Kennedy, who was a U.S. senator from Massachusetts. The other individual was Republican candidate Richard M. Nixon, the incumbent vice president in the administration of President Dwight D. Eisenhower. Kennedy and Nixon each sought Robinson's support in the election. Robinson continued to be a strong influence in the African American community, and the two candidates believed that his endorsement might win them votes from black voters. Robinson took the time to study their records and met with each man.

Following the meetings, Robinson said he was bothered that Kennedy seemed to know little about the African American community. Nixon's record on civil rights was not strong either, but Robinson considered it preferable to Kennedy's experience. Robinson announced that he would support Nixon's bid for the presidency. Kennedy, however, won the election (capturing a majority of the African American vote). As president, Kennedy initiated some of the most important civil rights advancements in U.S. history. (Nixon would win the presidency in 1968.)

Years after his first political endorsement, Robinson looked back on his choice. "I do not consider my decision to back Richard Nixon over John F. Kennedy for the presidency in 1960 one of my finer ones. It was a sincere one, however, at the time . . . As vice president and as presiding officer of the Senate, [Nixon] had a fairly good track record on civil rights . . . I found Mr. Kennedy a courteous man, obviously striving to please, but, just as obviously, uncomfortable as he sought to get a conversation going with me. It is remarkable how seemingly minor factors can influence a decision,"[1] Robinson wrote in 1972.

Robinson admitted he was disturbed that, in his 1960 meeting with Nixon, the vice president avoided the question of whether he would name an African American to his Cabinet if he was elected president. Robinson was also bothered that Nixon would not voice support for Martin Luther King, Jr. King was an African American Baptist minister and the main leader of the civil rights movement in the United States during the 1950's and 1960's. Around the time of the meeting, King was held in jail for a minor traffic violation in Georgia. Robinson noted that while he publicly continued to support Nixon, he was impressed that Kennedy used his political influence to quickly free King from jail.

HALL OF FAMER

In 1962, Robinson was voted into the National Baseball Hall of Fame in Cooperstown, New York. He had needed at least 75 percent of the ballots cast, or 120 votes, to be elected. Baseball writers gave him 77.5 percent of the vote, or 124 out of 160 ballots cast. On July 23, 1962, Robinson became the first African American enshrined in the Hall of Fame. During his speech, he had his wife, Rachel, his mother, Mallie, and his mentor, Branch Rickey, join him on stage. For decades, black ballplayers were not allowed to play with their white counterparts. Robinson had changed that, and now his plaque would be with those of all the other baseball greats.

In the early 1960's, Robinson was becoming restless in his job at Chock Full O'Nuts. He wanted to do more to help African Americans in the United States. After giving it much thought, he informed his bosses in 1964 that he would be leaving their company and accepting a new position with Nelson Rockefeller, the governor of New York. Rockefeller was a leader of the more liberal faction of the Republican Party and had contended for the party's presidential nomination in 1960.

Robinson had first met Rockefeller as a result of his political activities in 1960. Robinson also knew that the governor's family, which was very wealthy, donated large sums of money to African American causes and educational institutions. In 1964, Rockefeller contacted Robinson and asked him to become one of six deputy national directors in his second campaign for the Republican Party's presidential nomination. Because of his respect for Rockefeller, Robinson accepted and embarked on a new role in the political arena.

Rockefeller lost the Republican Party nomination to Barry Goldwater, who was a U.S. senator from Arizona. Throughout the campaign, Robinson had become increasingly uncomfortable with the growing dominance of the conservative wing of the Republican Party, but he remained close to Rockefeller. In 1966, Robinson was appointed as Governor Rockefeller's special assistant for community affairs in the state of New York.

For decades, black ballplayers were not allowed to play with their white counterparts. Robinson had changed that, and now his plaque would be with those of all the other baseball greats.

By 1968, Richard Nixon was again the Republican candidate for president of the United States. Robinson was still bothered by his support of Nixon eight years earlier. He decided that he would support Nixon's Democratic Party challenger, Hubert H. Humphrey. Humphrey, a former senator from Minnesota, was at the time vice president under President Lyndon B. Johnson.

As much as Robinson admired Rockefeller as a person, he believed that by the late 1960's, the Democratic Party had done more to assist the civil rights movement than had the Republican Party. Once again, though, Robinson's endorsement in a presidential election did little to elect his candidate, and Nixon defeated Humphrey.

CIVIL RIGHTS AMBASSADOR

On July 23, 1962, Robinson became the first African American elected to the National Baseball Hall of Fame.

Politics was not Robinson's only interest after hanging up his baseball uniform. He also became an influential voice in the growing civil rights movement. Robinson had helped change the face of baseball in the 1940's and 1950's; perhaps he could now help improve race relations in other areas of society. Robinson knew this would not be an easy undertaking.

The 1950's were the beginning of a difficult, divisive time in the United States. Racial segregation and discrimination had been part of everyone's lives for decades, but that was now all about to change. The roots of this change can be traced back to the early 1900's.

During World War I (1914–1918), orders for military equipment created a huge demand for labor, which led to mass black migration from rural areas in the South to manufacturing centers in the North. Once in the northern cities, African Americans found life was not as restrictive there as it had been in their Southern hometowns. Partly as a result of this migration, African Americans, starting in the 1930's, gained increasing prominence in politics and fairer hearings in federal courts.

Men such as Jackie Robinson and Branch Rickey made huge strides toward equality for the races in the 1940's and 1950's. But this change did not come overnight. In fact, many people thought that change was coming much too slowly.

In the early 1950's, the U.S. armed forces were still growing used to the idea of integration. In 1948, President Harry S. Truman had issued an executive order that all branches of the armed services be *desegregated*—that is, that white and black troops stop being separated by race. In part, President Truman's order read that "there shall be equality of treatment and opportunity for all persons in the armed services without regard to race, color, religion or national origin."[2]

In 1954, the Supreme Court of the United States ruled that racial segregation in public schools was unconstitutional. The Supreme Court's decision launched the legal movement to desegregate U.S. society. The full name of the case that helped change the course of history was *Brown et al. v. Board of Education of Topeka, Shawnee County, Kansas*. Many people commonly call it "Brown v. Board of Education."

SHARING A DREAM WITH MARTIN LUTHER KING

In 1955, Martin Luther King, Jr., led a protest against the segregation of the bus system in Montgomery, Alabama. A black passenger named Rosa Parks had been arrested for disobeying a city law requiring that blacks give up their seats on buses when white people wanted to sit in their seats or in the same row. Black leaders in Montgomery urged blacks to *boycott* (refuse to use) the city's buses. The leaders formed an organization to run the boycott and asked King to serve as president. In one of his speeches, King said that he did not support violence, but rather the right to protest.

King and other black ministers founded the Southern Christian Leadership Conference (SCLC) in 1957 to expand the nonviolent struggle against racism and discrimination. Robinson and King eventually became friends through the civil rights movement. The two men admired one another. They both shared the same dream—that of a United States in which blacks and whites were equals in everything. Whenever he could, Robinson would lend his help to King and the SCLC. However, Robinson—a man who always felt compelled to act to make things right—sometimes desired more aggressive action against racial injustice than King was willing to take.

As a result, Robinson often aligned himself with the National Association for the Advancement of Colored People (NAACP), another civil rights organization in the United States. This organization used legal and legislative measures to pursue its goal of racial equality. The NAACP played an important role in Brown v. Board of Education. (Thurgood Marshall, an attorney for the NAACP Legal Defense and Educational Fund, presented the argument in the case. Marshall would become the first African American Supreme Court justice in 1967.)

Robinson liked the fact that the NAACP took direct action to change the world. In 1956, the leadership of the NAACP awarded Robinson the Spingarn Medal. The Spingarn Medal, an annual award instituted by the NAACP in 1914, is presented in recognition of black Americans who have reached the highest levels of achievement in their chosen fields.

In late 1956, the leaders of the NAACP asked Robinson to take an active leadership role in the organization. Robinson accepted the challenge. His first assignment was to chair the annual NAACP Freedom Fund Drive in 1957. As the event chairman, Robinson traveled across the United States speaking at organization chapters to raise money for the NAACP. Robinson studied the facts involved in the many issues related to race relations and used them in his impassioned speeches to the public. He enjoyed the challenge of persuading people to support his point of view, and he committed himself to the work. At the end of his fund-raising campaign, the baseball legend had helped raise $1 million (about $7 million today). Because of his success in fund-raising, the NAACP elected Robinson to its National Board of Directors in late 1957.

Robinson never claimed much credit for the successes of the NAACP. Although he relied on his celebrity status to a certain extent, he also downplayed the importance of his role. However, he firmly believed that his work with the NAACP was helping the United States become a stronger nation. "I just happen to believe that American democracy is the business of every American. The NAACP has done a wonderful job, not only in the interest of the Negro people, but in the interest of American democracy,"[3] he wrote.

In 1958 and 1959, Robinson joined King and other African Americans in the "Youth March for Integrated Schools" in Washington, D.C., to protest the slow pace of school integration in the United States. Also in 1959, Robinson became the host of a radio interview program and began writing a newspaper column for the *New York Post*. The newspaper editors let him write about any topic that was of interest to him. He usually chose to write about civil rights, education, housing, illegal drugs, politics, or youth violence.

In 1962, Robinson began writing a column for the *Amsterdam News*. This was a small African American newspaper published in New York City.

Many people did not like what Robinson wrote in his columns. They disliked that this famous baseball player had become a civil rights advocate. Some people threatened to stop buying the *New York Post*. Others phoned Robinson's bosses at Chock Full O' Nuts, threatening to stop purchasing the company's products.

Robinson met several times with Martin Luther King, Jr., the most prominent leader of the civil rights movement in the United States in the 1960's.

Robinson's bosses at the company assured him that he was free to keep writing whatever he wanted. They said that if people were that upset about his columns, they could go buy some other brand of coffee.

In May 1963, Robinson traveled to Birmingham, Alabama, to join King's efforts to achieve desegregation in that city. Birmingham was very resistant to civil rights changes. Many demonstrations became violent, and both demonstrators and innocent bystanders were injured. What Robinson saw angered him. Although some fans and ballplayers had treated him poorly when he was a player, he could not believe that people would be as violent as they were in the Birmingham demonstrations. His anger intensified in September, when a group of white men bombed a church in Birmingham, killing four little girls. It was clear to Robinson that the United States still had a long way to go before all its citizens would be treated equally.

In June 1963, the Robinson family hosted a jazz concert on the front lawn of their Connecticut home to raise money for the SCLC. The family continued to host such concerts throughout the 1960's.

In the early 1960's, many black people became interested in opening their own businesses. Unfortunately, many banks refused to give them the loans they needed to get started. In 1964, Robinson helped organize Freedom National Bank in New York City's Harlem neighborhood. He also helped raise about $1 million to enable the bank to open its doors. The bank was owned and operated by a group of African American community leaders and investors. Just as Robinson had provided new opportunities for African Americans in baseball, he was now opening new channels for them to enter the business world.

Chapter 8: Changing Times

Robinson found that by the late 1960's he was growing uneasy with some aspects of civil rights organizations in the United States. Since becoming involved in the movement, Robinson did not feel comfortable around civil rights activists who were too conservative or those who were too militant. Sitting back and doing nothing would never change the world. However, violence would risk destroying what he and others had worked so hard to accomplish. In the late 1960's, Robinson felt that some advocates of civil rights were being too aggressive, and he often found himself taking different viewpoints from the more militant black leaders.

One of these militant African American leaders was Malcolm X, a fiery speaker who often encouraged blacks to live separately from whites and to win their freedom "by any means necessary." Malcolm X rejected nonviolence as a principle. However, he did seek cooperation with King and other civil rights activists who favored nonviolent protests. Malcolm X was assassinated in 1965, but not before he and Robinson had publicly disagreed on several racial issues.

In 1972, Robinson published his autobiography, *I Never Had It Made*. He had earlier written two other books about his life and baseball career. In *I Never Had It Made*, he tried to express some of his feelings about Malcolm X and the civil rights movement:

> *Although I had disagreed with Malcolm intensely on many issues . . . I rated him as articulate, incredibly sharp, and intelligent. Despite our differences, I realized that he projected a great image for young black kids who needed virile black males to emulate. Because he had been in prison, had associated with whores and dope addicts, and had come out of it to prove that people can rise from the depths, Malcolm had a strong appeal for youngsters that lasted far beyond his death.*[1]

Elijah Muhammad was another activist of the era whose viewpoints differed from Robinson's ideals. Muhammad was the major leader of the original Nation of Islam, whose members called themselves Black Muslims. This organization combined religious beliefs with black nationalism. Unlike Robinson, Muhammad favored racial separation and wanted to establish a black nation within the United States.

In 1967, Robinson announced that he would resign from his position on the NAACP board. He believed its leadership had cut itself off from promising moderate leaders in the civil rights struggle.

The world—including the world of civil rights—was changing. Robinson's life was about to undergo tremendous change, too.

Jackie Robinson's personal life often was in upheaval during the 1960's. In 1965, Branch Rickey, the Dodgers owner who had become like a father to him, died. The pair had developed a deep personal relationship, and Robinson missed his old friend. Then,

A group of picketers demanding more jobs for African Americans at a construction site in New York City gets a little help from Robinson in August 1963.

in 1968, Robinson's mother died in California. Like many mothers, she had made a great many sacrifices so that her son could be a success in his life. Now she was gone, yet he took some comfort in knowing that he had worked hard to make her proud.

Meanwhile, Robinson was facing an internal struggle involving his wife, Rachel, and one of their children. Rachel Robinson wanted to resume her career after their youngest child started school full-time. But like many men in the 1950's and 1960's, Jackie Robinson believed that wives should stay at home. He remembered that his own mother was rarely home because she was forced to work to keep her family fed. He did not want his own children to lack a mother at home. The family had enough money and they were living a very comfortable life style, so why would his wife want to work?

For Rachel, the issue was not money. She wanted to be more than the wife of a celebrity. Eventually, she persuaded her husband to see her point of view. She enrolled at New York University, obtained a master's degree in psychiatric nursing, and went to work at a hospital in New York City. She eventually became a professor at Yale University in New Haven, Connecticut, instructing new nursing students on the care of patients.

INTERNAL STRUGGLES

Rachel Robinson's desire to "be her own person" indicated to her husband that the family was being affected by his fame—and not always in a good way. One of the couple's sons, Jack Jr., had a very difficult time dealing with the pressure. Jack hated to talk about his father's baseball career. He also probably had an undiagnosed learning disability. He would argue with his parents, brother, and sister, often feeling like an outsider in his own family. Jack eventually dropped out of high school. Jackie Robinson, a man who had spoken to millions of people, was frustrated that he did not seem to know how to talk with his own son.

In 1964, Jack Jr., enlisted in the U.S. Army, where he served for three years. He was sent to fight in the Vietnam War (1957–1975). Wounded in combat while in Vietnam, he received the Purple

Heart, a medal given to members of the armed forces who have been wounded or killed in action.

Jack returned home from Vietnam a confused young man. He became addicted to drugs and got into trouble with the police. His parents eventually placed him in a drug treatment center where he would get the help he needed.

By 1971, Robinson's son had freed himself from his drug addiction and had a job working at the rehabilitation clinic that had helped him. Father and son were also communicating better than they ever had before. Sadly, on June 17, 1971, Jack, Jr., was killed when his car skidded off the road.

The tragedy was the latest in a series of personal troubles for Robinson, who was in failing health. It seems paradoxical that a man like Jackie Robinson—someone who had lettered in four sports in college and played professional baseball for a decade—would have serious health problems at a relatively young age. Yet this is exactly what Robinson faced beginning in the 1960's. Although only in his 40's, he suffered a heart attack in 1968. He had another in 1970. He also had high blood pressure and *diabetes mellitus,* which was diagnosed shortly after he left the Dodgers. Diabetes mellitus is a long-term disease that disrupts the body's ability to use a sugar called glucose. The disease can result in a number of serious complications.

By 1972, diabetes had cost Robinson the vision in one eye and caused the vision in his other eye to become severely blurred. He could no longer read or write. Fans continued to write him letters, however, offering words of encouragement.

BEYOND THE WORLD OF SPORTS

In his 1972 autobiography, Robinson recalled being left speechless by a telegram that had been sent to a New York City newspaper. The person who sent the telegram, an African American woman from Detroit, asked that it be published in the hope that Robinson would see it. The woman wrote, "Jackie, I read in the *Free Press* [a Detroit newspaper] this morning that you've lost sight in your right eye and [your vision] is very bad in the left. Do you think a transplant will help? I will be glad to give you one of mine. You can call me at work between 8:15 and 5:30 PM."[2]

Although Robinson did not accept the woman's incredibly charitable offer, he was touched to know that the public still cared so deeply for him. The woman's words spurred Robinson to continue traveling the country to give speeches and to promote civil rights causes. Her offer also helped him see that his efforts were not in vain. In his book, he noted that the outpouring of support he had received from fans—and hopes of further action toward racial equality—inspired him to continue his fight.

According to Robinson, "There have been some meaningful public demonstrations recently that made me realize people see that I have attempted to make a contribution beyond the world of sports. I have always fought for my principles and spoken out for my ideals. Recognition coming at this time has given me the determination to live as many more productive years as I can."[3]

> *"There have been some meaningful public demonstrations recently that made me realize people see that I have attempted to make a contribution beyond the world of sports."*
>
> Jackie Robinson, 1972

Through the years, Robinson had become friends with Jesse Jackson, a dynamic African American civil rights activist, minister, and political leader. Jackson had been one of King's associates at the SCLC when he first met Robinson. Jackson left the SCLC to establish a new organization, People United to Save Humanity (PUSH), in 1972. He invited Robinson to join PUSH as its first vice president, a role Robinson was proud to accept.

The year 1972 also marked the 25th anniversary of the breaking of baseball's color barrier. Despite his own poor health, Robinson marked the anniversary by attending a special ceremony in June 1972 at Dodger Stadium in Los Angeles. At the ceremony, the Dodgers honored Robinson by *retiring* his uniform number, 42 (meaning that this number could never be used again by another player on the team).

Robinson was also invited to throw out the first pitch during the second game of the 1972 World Series in Cincinnati, Ohio. On Oct. 15, 1972, the Cincinnati crowd watched Robinson throw the ceremonial first pitch. Countless other fans watched on television. In what would be his last public speech, Robinson seized the opportunity to address the subject of racial diversity in the game he played.

"I am extremely proud and pleased. I'm going to be more pleased and more proud when I look at that third-base coaching line one day and see a black face managing in baseball,"[4] he said. (Frank Robinson, no relation to Jackie Robinson, became the first African American to manage a major league ball club when he took over the helm of the Cleveland Indians in 1975.)

Jackie Robinson had a renewed vigor and determination to live, but illness had taken its toll on his body. In addition to all his other health problems, his physicians told him before his World Series appearance that they were considering amputating his leg. Despite this bad news, he managed to joke at the World Series game with Pee Wee Reese, his former teammate, that he would obtain an artificial leg, learn how to walk on it, then challenge his old friend to a game of golf and still be able to beat him.

Robinson never got that chance. On Oct. 24, 1972, he was at home in Stamford when he suffered another heart attack and collapsed. An ambulance arrived immediately to take him to the hospital, but he died on the way there.

Thousands of people—black, white, and of other races—lined the streets of Harlem along Robinson's funeral procession on October 29. Many of his former teammates attended the funeral to show their respect. His pallbearers included Bill Russell, a basketball player for the Boston Celtics, and former Brooklyn Dodgers teammates Joe Black, Ralph Branca, Jim "Junior" Gilliam, Don Newcombe, and Pee Wee Reese.

The Reverend Jesse Jackson delivered the eulogy at the funeral, noting that Robinson had "turned the stumbling block into a stepping stone" in his life and career, and that his breaking of baseball's color barrier helped lead the way to racial desegregation in the United States. Jackson added that Robinson's bravery on

the playing field created "ripples of possibility,"[5] which were confirmed just a few years later in such legal decisions as Brown v. Board of Education.

THE LEGACY OF JACKIE ROBINSON

Years after his death, people still fondly recall Jackie Robinson. In 1973, his family and friends created the Jackie Robinson Foundation, an organization that provides education and leadership-development opportunities for young people with the expectation that they, in turn, will find ways to assist their communities. In 1984, President Ronald Reagan posthumously awarded Jackie Robinson the Presidential Medal of Freedom in recognition of his courage and bravery. The Medal of Freedom, the highest civilian honor in the United States, is awarded by the president for outstanding public service.

In 1997, on the 50th anniversary of the day Robinson broke the color barrier, major league baseball executives announced that they would retire the number 42 from the game. That meant that no player on any team in either the American League or National

League would again wear Robinson's number. Next to being elected to the Baseball Hall of Fame, this is the highest honor bestowed upon a ballplayer.

In her 2004 book, *Promises To Keep*, Robinson's daughter Sharon reflected on her father and his accomplishments:

> *Dad spent his entire life fighting for equality. He won some battles and lost others. He made some mistakes, but he also inspired millions. My father never lost hope or gave in to despair, even when his health failed him.*[6]

The epitaph on Jackie Robinson's headstone also speaks volumes about the man, eloquently summing up his amazing experience and philosophy on living. The quote, attributed to the Hall of Famer, reads simply, "A life is not important except in the impact it has on other lives."[7]

Those words are a fitting tribute to a man whose life continues to have an impact on generations of people. ■

The epitaph on Robinson's headstone sums up his philosophy of life.

Branch Rickey (1881–1965)

Branch Rickey is best remembered as the man who engineered the integration of major league baseball when he signed Jackie Robinson, an African American, to the Brooklyn Dodgers in 1947. Rickey may well have earned his niche in the Baseball Hall of Fame even had he not shattered baseball's color barrier by being the first modern major league general manager to sign an African American player. Nicknamed "the Mahatma" (wise man) of baseball, Rickey was a visionary who developed the stratified minor league baseball network, in which players develop their skills in minor league "farm teams" before moving up to the majors. This system, which is still in use today, knits together the entirety of professional baseball into a dynamic and organized structure.

ROOTING FOR THE RED STOCKINGS

Wesley Branch Rickey was born on Dec. 20, 1881, in Stockdale, Ohio. He was the second of three sons born to Jacob and Emily Rickey. In 1883, the family moved to a farm near Lucasville, Ohio. Education and religion were key elements of Rickey's formative years. Rickey's parents wanted their child to have a better life than they had themselves. As a result, Jacob Rickey endeavored to fill their home with books. When the bookstore in the nearby town of Portsmouth burned, the elder Rickey made a roundtrip journey to purchase as many damaged but usable books as he could afford. He was able to purchase a new family Bible, as well as books on art, natural history, and literature.

As a child, Rickey enjoyed his evenings spent reading more than he did his days tending to his chores on the family farm. He also attended a one-room schoolhouse near the farm. In 1892, the Rickeys moved to a house in Lucasville, in part because the parents wanted their sons to continue their education at a larger school in town.

School life in Lucasville got off to a rocky start. Rickey's classmates teased him about his rural upbringing. His self-consciousness began to overwhelm him, and Rickey developed a stutter. One of his teachers, however, saw the potential that was inside the new student and acted as a mentor. By the end of his first year, Rickey was showing signs of becoming a great speaker. Around this time, Wesley Branch Rickey decided that he would now be called Branch Rickey to avoid confusion with two cousins who shared the same first name.

Working on a farm was more difficult than studying at school. After a few days spent plowing fields, Rickey told his parents he was ready to finish his education.

In 1895, Rickey decided that it was time to repay his parents for encouraging him to pursue an education rather than work the family farm. He quit school and announced that he would be returning to work on their farm in Lucasville. Working on a farm, however, was much more difficult than studying at school. After a few days spent plowing fields, Rickey told his parents he was ready to finish his education.

The following summer, he spent time with his older brother, Orla, who was home from his job as a teacher. Orla's true passion was the summertime pursuit of baseball. He primarily enjoyed following the fortunes of the Cincinnati (Ohio) Red Stockings. (This professional ball club was the first major league baseball team. Formed in 1869, the team eventually shortened its name to the more familiar Cincinnati Reds.)

Branch often played baseball with his brother. Emily Rickey even made homemade baseballs for her sons. The boys would use the balls when playing the game on the weekends. Orla became the star pitcher on the local Lucasville baseball squad, while Branch played as catcher.

Discovering baseball was not the only change that came over Rickey when he lived in Lucasville. During his teen years, he fell in love with Jane Moulton, a girl he had known since childhood. In 1898, 16-year-old Jane left to study at the Western College for Women in Oxford, Ohio. Jane and Branch then began writing frequent letters to each other.

While Rickey entertained thoughts of love, he also was concerned about his own future. He studied for and passed the county examination to qualify to work as a grammar school teacher. In 1899, he accepted a job teaching at a one-room school in Turkey Creek, Ohio. In 1900, Rickey made a momentous decision—to attend Ohio Wesleyan University (OWU) in Delaware, Ohio. His friends and family were not surprised, because they had always been impressed by Rickey's intelligence. In March 1901, Rickey began his new life as a college student.

Once commenting on the six-hour train ride from Lucasville to Delaware, Ohio, Rickey said, "I wanted to go to college more than anything else in the world, and I didn't care how I got there. I just wanted to go."[1]

While at college, Rickey seized the opportunity to join OWU's athletic teams. He played baseball in the spring and football in the autumn. Rickey knew many of the players on his college teams from teams he played with in Lucasville.

In the fall of 1901, Rickey enrolled in the maximum number of classes permitted by OWU. His old pen pal, Jane Moulton, was also at the university. The pair would spend as much time together as his busy schedule (and strict early 1900's codes of conduct) permitted.

Returning home in the summer of 1902, Rickey found work as a catcher for the Portsmouth Navvies, a semiprofessional baseball club. Earning $25 (about $560 today) a game, he traveled through the Southern United States, playing a number of games before returning to school that fall. As it turned out, his acceptance of payment for playing baseball would affect his days as a rising college star.

Upon his return to OWU, several newspaper articles noted that because he had accepted money from the Navvies, his membership on any college team would violate a new rule prohibiting athletes who received payment for playing sports from playing on college teams. The new rule was part of an agreement drawn up by officials of several Ohio colleges and universities that summer. Although the agreement was not ratified by all the schools until autumn—after Rickey had left the Navvies and returned to school—it was still applied to Rickey. To try to save Rickey's college playing career, the owner of the Navvies claimed that Rickey had never been paid, but Rickey admitted to having been paid and accepted his ineligibility.

Now kept off of OWU's baseball and football teams, Rickey found time to join the semiprofessional Shelby (Ohio) Steel Tube Company football team. Rickey was paid $50 (about $1,120 today) a game and drew on his experience from the OWU squad to assist in coaching. His football days were sidelined in the third game of the season, however, when he broke his ankle.

COACH RICKEY

When he was 21 years old, Rickey was offered the chance to coach OWU's baseball team. Rickey had proved himself to be a hardworking student and an upstanding young man by being truthful about his experience with the Navvies. The university administration believed it was time to reward him for his honesty—and to benefit from his knowledge of the game.

While coaching the OWU team in 1903, Rickey got a firsthand look at racial *segregation* (the separation of people because of race) in the world around him. One of the players on his team was Charles Thomas, a young African American student whom Rickey had met shortly after Thomas's arrival at the school. In a scheduled home game against a school from Kentucky, the Southern players were shocked to see an African American player on the Ohio team. They also began shouting racially insensitive remarks toward Thomas and the rest of the OWU team. Moreover, the Southern team demanded that the umpire remove Thomas from the playing field. Rickey, however, refused to take his friend out of the game.

The following spring, the team traveled to South Bend, Indiana, to play the University of Notre Dame baseball team. The OWU team had reservations at a local hotel, but when they entered the lobby, the hotel clerk was surprised to see Thomas traveling with the rest of the team. The clerk informed Rickey that the hotel allowed only white guests and that Thomas could not stay there. Rickey was stunned and very upset. He wondered, how could one person treat another person so callously?

The hotel finally agreed to let Thomas share a room with Rickey, but the young player was hurt by the experience. Rickey later recalled how, in their room, he saw Thomas fighting tears and rubbing his hands, lamenting the color of his own skin.[2]

Rickey vowed that night to always do whatever he could to see that other African Americans did not have to face the bitter indignity that Thomas faced at the hands of racism. Little did Rickey know the historic role he would one day play in the evolution of civil rights in the United States.

In 1904, Branch Rickey graduated from Ohio Wesleyan University and returned to his family's home in Lucasville. With the hope of earning enough money to further his education and obtain a law degree, Rickey accepted an offer of $175 (about $3,780 today) a month to play baseball for a team in Texas. A short time later, news of his catching ability reached the owners of the Cincinnati Reds, Rickey's "hometown" heroes. Rickey accepted their invitation to join their team.

The excitement of joining the Cincinnati Reds was short-lived. Rickey informed the team owners that he had promised his mother that, for religious reasons, he would not play baseball on Sundays. In fact, he said he would not even carry his equipment if Sunday was a travel day for the team. (In later years, he would have a contract stipulation that he would not play on Sundays.)

The Cincinnati Reds organization was dismayed by Rickey's position. Although Rickey had been highly recommended, the team manager, Joe Kelley, cut him from the team before he ever played a regular game.

BASEBALL HONEYMOON

Despite his time on the road traveling for baseball, Rickey's relationship with Jane Moulton continued to intensify. With his baseball career apparently over, Rickey accepted a position as a teacher, mostly of literature classes, and an athletic coach at a small college in Pennsylvania. Letters between the couple turned to the subject of marriage and, in 1905, Jane and Rickey announced their plans to marry.

Rickey told his bride-to-be that he planned to fulfill his long-time dream of enrolling in law school. However, news then came that the St. Louis Browns, a major league baseball team in Missouri, was interested in signing him as a catcher. After discussing the matter with Jane, they agreed that he would play for only one year to earn money for law school.

In his first year in the big leagues, Rickey played in only one game with three at-bats before returning home because his mother was ill. Despite his original agreement with Jane, he returned to the team the following season.

On June 1, 1906, after eight years of writing letters and dating, Branch Rickey and Jane Moulton were married at her parents' home in Lucasville. During their marriage they would have six children: Mary, Branch Jr., Jane, Alice, Elizabeth, and Sue.

The Rickeys' honeymoon consisted of a road trip with the St. Louis Browns. There were stops in such cities as Boston, Chicago, New York, and Washington, D.C. The newlyweds eventually made their home in a new apartment in St. Louis.

During the 1906 season, Rickey recorded his best year as a player, seeing action in 65 games with a .284 *batting average*. (Batting average shows the percentage of times that a player gets a base hit. It is the number of hits divided by the number of official times that the player has been at bat.) In 1907, the Browns traded their young backup catcher to the New York Highlanders, a team that would soon change its name to the New York Yankees.

Rickey batted only .182 with the Highlanders. His luck behind the plate was even worse than it was in the batter's box. During

Rickey played with the New York Highlanders in 1907.

one game against the Washington Senators, Rickey was catching when the Senators stole 13 bases. He was unable to throw any of these runners out. After such a dismal showing (and after being diagnosed with an injured throwing arm), Rickey decided to leave baseball at the end of the season.

During baseball's off-seasons, Rickey had coached football and baseball at OWU , where he earned a second bachelor's degree. By the end of 1907, he was working during the day at the YMCA in Delaware, Ohio, as an administrative secretary, and taking law courses at night at Ohio State University.

In 1909, Rickey enrolled full time at the University of Michigan Law School at Ann Arbor. When the university's athletic coach resigned, Rickey applied for and got the job—though some professors warned him that being a full-time law student and a coach was too much for any one person. Nevertheless,

Rickey earned his law degree in two years in a program that typically took three years to complete.

Rickey and two classmates decided to form a law firm together in Idaho, so the Rickeys packed their bags and moved to Boise. The practice turned out to be less than profitable, and Rickey decided to return to Ann Arbor for the spring to coach baseball. It was now obvious that baseball was replacing law as Rickey's true calling.

BASEBALL MANAGER

In 1913, Rickey coached his last season at the University of Michigan. The owner of the St. Louis Browns had invited Rickey back to the team. This time, however, it would not be as a player. The team's management asked Rickey to join the club as the assistant to the president. In this position, he would be able to combine his knowledge of baseball with his legal ability and skills as an *orator* (speaker). The latter skill was important because the job required him to be a persuasive speaker. He took the job, believing it to be the best of both worlds.

Rickey stayed with the Browns from 1913 to 1915. One of his star players was pitcher George Sisler, who later became one of the most famous players of his era and was voted into the Baseball Hall of Fame. (The Baseball Hall of Fame, in Cooperstown, New York, honors individuals who have made significant contributions to baseball.) Toward the end of the 1913 season, Rickey took over as the team's field manager. Under Rickey's management in 1914, the Browns posted a record of 71-82 (meaning the team won 71 games and lost 82). For a few games that year, Rickey even decided to take some turns at bat as a player. Unfortunately, his return as a player did not turn the team around.

Things got worse for the Browns the following season, when the team's record fell to 63-91. It was a lackluster return to the dugout, and Rickey realized his time was better spent behind a desk. A new owner decided the team needed a different field manager in 1916, but Rickey continued his work in the Browns organization as business manager.

Branch Rickey was a man who always enjoyed a challenge. So, when the crosstown rival St. Louis Cardinals offered him a chance to serve as the ball club's president, he accepted the offer. He stayed at that job from 1917 to 1918, when he left to serve in the U.S. military in France during the last few months of World War I (1914–1918).

Returning to the Cardinals in January 1919, he not only worked in the front office, but he took on the additional role as the team's field manager. Rickey returned to the game he loved, but the Cardinals won just 54 games that season. He posted his best managerial record to date in 1921, when he led the team to an 87-66 record, with help from players like future Hall of Famer Rogers Hornsby, who hit .397 that year.

It was in the role of general manager of the St. Louis Cardinals that the executive side of Rickey began showing some of the brilliance that would make baseball history.

In the middle of the 1925 season, the team ownership replaced Rickey as field manager after the Cardinals got off to a weak 13-25 start. Hornsby, the Cardinals' star player, succeeded Rickey as player-manager and led St. Louis to an overall 77-76 record that season.

Rickey was dejected by the turn of events. But as it turned out, Rickey simply had traded in his baseball cap for yet another position—general manager of the St. Louis Cardinals. It was in this role that the executive side of Rickey began showing some of the brilliance that would make baseball history.

EXECUTIVE BRANCH

During the 1920's and 1930's, Rickey created the *farm system,* in which the talents of young ballplayers could be cultivated and refined. (The name "farm system" was coined after someone referred to the concept as "farming out" potential big league players to minor league teams.) The best players would rise to the top and find their way to the major leagues. Those of limited playing ability would remain in the minor leagues. The Cardinals purchased a number of minor league teams in which they could train and develop talented players discovered by the organization's *scouts* (people sent out to get information about athletes or athletic teams).

The farm system was originally developed only for the Cardinals. Before long, however, all major league teams copied the idea and used it to develop their own young talent. The concept continues to work very well for major league teams today. Famous players of the 1920's and 1930's, including Dizzy Dean, Johnny Mize, and Enos Slaughter, honed their craft in the farm system before making their major league debuts.

Rickey hired retired big league players to return as coaches, managers, and scouts to teach the young players in the farm system. One of the men he hired as a scout in 1926 was his younger brother, Frank. The younger Rickey had no playing experience. Instead, he was a former sheriff and agent for the Federal Bureau of Investigation. Regardless, he stayed with the St. Louis team for almost 20 years and also briefly worked for the New York Giants, Brooklyn Dodgers, and Pittsburgh Pirates. Frank Rickey signed such famous players as Marty Marion, Johnny Mize, Preacher Roe, and Enos Slaughter.

Professional baseball began to thrive as a result of the farm club system. Before long, more talented players were making it to the majors. The Cardinals especially benefited from the concept, becoming one of the most successful franchises in the National League. Rickey's efforts helped baseball grow during an otherwise bleak period in U.S. history called the *Great Depression* (a period of economic hardship that began in 1929 and lasted throughout the 1930's). While at the helm of the Cardinals, Rickey also began mentoring other young executives, including Warren Giles, who would later become president of the National League.

DODGERS PRESIDENT AND GENERAL MANAGER

The world began changing dramatically in the 1940's. The Great Depression was over, but the United States now found itself in World War II (1939-1945). In 1942, life changed for Branch Rickey, too. At age 61 and after 25 years with the St. Louis Cardinals, he accepted a job as president and general manager of the Brooklyn Dodgers. Soon after starting the job, he also became part owner of the ball club.

Rickey tried to think of ways to turn the struggling Brooklyn Dodgers into a winning team. As he did with the Cardinals, he started by grooming young players in the farm club system for future seasons with the Dodgers. With World War II raging overseas, many other baseball teams had scaled back their scouting operations. They were afraid that any players they signed might be drafted to serve in the armed forces. Rickey was more aggressive and, with little competition, was able to sign many of the best players available.

Since his days as a college baseball coach, Rickey had been quick to experiment with new ideas to help improve his players and teams. He had developed such training ideas as the *batting cage* (a screen placed behind the batter to stop baseballs during batting practice), the pitching machine, and the batting helmet. As Dodgers general manager, Rickey had one idea that he thought might help turn the Dodgers into a winning team while giving many talented players their first opportunity to play major league ball. However, he kept this idea a secret from everyone but his closest associates. The idea had to be kept secret because it broke an unwritten, but generally accepted, rule of baseball.

As general manager of the Brooklyn Dodgers in the 1940's, Rickey helped develop many young players.

Rickey sent his scouts across the United States and the Caribbean in search of talented players—talented *black* players.

Neither baseball's American League nor its National League had a written rule regarding segregation, but everyone involved in the sport knew about the "unwritten rule" prohibiting whites and blacks from being teammates. The rule dated back to the late 1800's and would last until 1947. Cap Anson, a player and manager in the late 1800's, reportedly was one of the main proponents of baseball segregation. At a time when the theory of "separate but equal" was spreading in American society, African American players became excluded from the major and minor leagues and confined to separate Negro leagues and teams.

We may never know the exact reason that Rickey wanted to integrate baseball. There have been many opinions expressed, however. Some baseball historians believe that Rickey was still haunted by the treatment of Charles Thomas that he had observed years earlier. Other historians maintain that Rickey's main motivation was helping the Dodgers win a pennant for the first time since 1920, and that by opening up the playing field to the untapped talent he had noted while scouting many African American players, he might improve the team's chances. Still others claim that Rickey envisioned a place for himself in baseball and civil rights history if his plan worked.

What we do know is that in 1943, a rumor began circulating that Rickey was planning to start a new Negro league team. He used this story as a cover to send scouts out in search of promising young black players.

THE "BROWN DODGERS"

Rickey knew that the Negro leagues had many talented players who were prevented from playing in the majors because of the color of their skin. Many of these players were well known and hoped their prominence would attract the attention of Rickey's scouts. These players included Satchel Paige, one of the greatest pitchers of all time.

Rickey studied the scouting reports and considered several

different players. Unfortunately, Paige was never in the running, primarily because of his age, but perhaps also because of his reputation for doing and saying whatever he wanted, whenever he wanted to.

One of the top prospects was Roy Campanella. Campanella was a catcher for the Baltimore (Maryland) Elite Giants of the Negro leagues from 1937 to 1942 and again from 1944 to 1945. His mother was black and his father was Italian. Although Rickey decided not to sign Campanella as the first black player in the modern major leagues, Campanella would eventually be signed by Rickey as the first black catcher in the major leagues.

In 1945, as a way of continuing to draw attention away from his true plan, Rickey announced his intention to create a team called the Brooklyn Brown Dodgers to play in a new Negro league called the United States League. Operating under the belief that they were filling roles for a team of all-black players, the Dodgers scouts now intensified their search.

Several scouts sent a report to Rickey about a player named Jackie Robinson. A former U.S. Army officer, Robinson was playing for the Kansas City Monarchs (alongside Satchel Paige) in 1945. Impressed by what he had learned from scouts and from Robinson's army record, Rickey believed Robinson to be a man who was not only a talented player but also capable of withstanding the stress of being the first black major league player. Rickey sent word to Robinson that he wanted to meet with him to discuss his joining a new baseball team.

In August 1945, Robinson traveled to New York City, still believing the team in question was the Brown Dodgers. At the start of their meeting, Rickey asked some questions about Robinson's family and background. Then, Rickey revealed his plan: He did not want Robinson for a new Negro league team; he wanted him to join the Brooklyn Dodgers.

Rickey warned Robinson about the kind of verbal abuse the player would have to take, using examples of crude racial taunts that players and fans might shout at him. They discussed the idea, and Robinson plainly asked Rickey if he was looking for "a Negro who is afraid to fight back."

"I'm looking for a ballplayer with guts enough not to fight back,"[3] Rickey replied.

BREAKING THE COLOR BARRIER

By the end of the meeting, the two men had agreed to work together to break baseball's color barrier, though the plan for Robinson to play with the Dodgers had to remain a secret a little while longer. In October 1945, Robinson signed a major league contract with the Montreal Royals, a minor league affiliate of the Brooklyn Dodgers. He joined the Royals in 1945, and helped his new team dominate the International League. On April 10, 1947, the Dodgers purchased Robinson's contract from the Royals and, on April 15, 1947, he became the first African American to play in the modern major leagues.

Rickey is shown in 1950 meeting with Jackie Robinson, whom he had signed in 1947 as the first African American to play modern major league baseball.

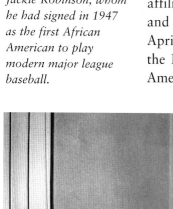

Reflecting on the historic role he played, Rickey wrote in his 1965 book, *The American Diamond: A Documentary of the Game of Baseball,* that everyone involved in the groundbreaking move was confident of its ultimate success. "It was never in anyone's mind that a competent Negro player could not be found. There were plenty of them. No doubt about that, and very soon Brooklyn, having several Negro players, went out of its way to see to it that Larry Doby, a fine major-leaguer, went to Cleveland. Brooklyn needed a partner to develop the process of Negro employment,"[4] he wrote.

In August 1947, just four months after Jackie Robinson took to the field, Cleveland Indians owner Bill Veeck signed Doby to a major league contract. He became the first African

American player in the American League. The following year, Veeck would also sign Paige, the Negro league legend, as the oldest *rookie* (first-season player) to join the majors.

For three years, Robinson kept a promise to Rickey to *"turn the other cheek"* when it came to insults. Although Robinson maintained his steely composure, it was not easy, because he was not the type of person who kept his opinions to himself. In 1949, Rickey told Robinson he was now on his own and free to choose his own battles. Robinson began to speak out about the need for the continued integration of major league teams. He also became one of the greatest second basemen ever to play the game.

For Rickey, 1950 was another year of change. That year, he left the Dodgers to join the Pittsburgh Pirates as vice president and general manager. Much of the ingenuity that had defined Rickey for his entire career, however, seemed to wane after his move. Despite his best efforts, he was unable to create a winning team. He remained vice president and general manager until 1955, when he was elevated to Pirates chairman of the board and director.

Although he was no longer hitting "home runs" as a baseball executive, Rickey was still an effective speaker and attorney. From 1957 to 1961, he served as vice chairman of the President's Committee on Government Employment Policy. President Dwight D. Eisenhower had established the committee to eliminate racial discrimination in the federal government.

NEW CHALLENGES

By 1959, Rickey had left Pittsburgh but not the baseball world. He set his sights on a new challenge—a third baseball league. It was to be called the Continental League and would be designed to fill the demand for baseball in non-major league baseball cities. Baseball historians maintain that the concept was not without merit. For example, baseball had not grown from the 16 original teams conceived in the early 1900's. The United States had grown tremendously, with a large population shift into the western portion of the country, but cities there lacked professional baseball teams.

The Continental League would have had franchises in Atlanta, Buffalo, Dallas-Fort Worth, Denver, Houston, Minneapolis-St. Paul, New York City, and Toronto. Eventually, new teams would have been added in Honolulu, Montreal, New Orleans, San Diego, and Seattle.

Rickey served as Continental League president from 1959 to 1962. The league, however, failed to get off the ground. It did succeed in affecting the game, however. Baseball historians credit it with inspiring major league baseball's expansion in 1961 and 1962 through the addition of the Houston Colt .45's (later renamed the Houston Astros), the Los Angeles Angels, the New York Mets, and the Washington (D.C.) Senators. (The owners of the original Senators, one of the first major league baseball teams, had relocated the organization at the end of the 1960 season, renaming the team the Minnesota Twins.) Some people wonder if expanding the existing major leagues had been Rickey's real plan all along.

Rickey suffered a personal loss in April 1961 when his only son, Branch Jr., died of hepatitis and complications from diabetes and pneumonia. Branch Jr. had been business manager for the St. Louis Cardinals, later becoming vice president in charge of minor league clubs for the Pittsburgh Pirates.

Rickey and his wife were devastated by their son's death. Rickey himself was already suffering from the effects of a variety of health ailments, and the shock to his system was almost too much to withstand. He suffered a heart attack two months later.

Rickey's spirits were lifted in 1962, when the Baseball Hall of Fame inducted Jackie Robinson into its hallowed ranks. Standing alongside Robinson was Rickey, who could not have been more proud of Robinson's achievement and recognition if he were his father.

FINAL TIME AT BAT

In 1962, the St. Louis Cardinals invited Rickey to rejoin the team as a senior consultant for player development. Rickey had first stet foot on Cardinals soil in 1917 and, by now, everyone he knew was long gone. Still, he was excited by the opportunity, though many of his friends and family believed that such an undefined role was little more than a publicity stunt for the Cardinals and would lead to disappointment for a man in his early 80's.

Some people in the Cardinals organization did not like the "old school" way that Rickey conducted business. They thought that he was too harsh and too up-front with his ideas. (At the end of the 1962 season, Rickey had suggested that future Hall of Famer Stan Musial, a St. Louis legend, should retire because age was beginning to slow him down. Musial had hit a respectable .330 that year.)

In 1964, the St. Louis Cardinals won the World Series by defeating the New York Yankees four games to three. Most people agreed, however, that Rickey played no part in that victory. Rickey believed himself unfairly blamed for whatever problems existed within the organization. Regardless, in October 1964, Rickey was let go as a team consultant.

In 1962, the Baseball Hall of Fame inducted Jackie Robinson into its hallowed ranks. Standing alongside Robinson was Branch Rickey, who could not have been more proud of Robinson's achievement and recognition if he were his father.

By the mid-1960's, Rickey had spent some 60 years involved in a sport he adored. His heart condition had grown worse and he was now confined to a wheelchair. Yet Rickey was happy to speak to groups of people whenever asked.

On Nov. 9, 1965, while delivering a speech in Columbus, Missouri, Rickey collapsed on stage. He died on December 9, 11 days shy of his 84th birthday. One of the most influential executives in baseball history was gone.

HALL OF FAME LEGACY

In 1967, Rickey was posthumously inducted into the Baseball Hall of Fame for his part in breaking baseball's color barrier and in recognition of his reputation as a skilled negotiator and effective baseball executive.

Rickey changed the face of major league baseball. Furthermore, through his decision to integrate the sport, he gave impetus to the civil rights movement in the United States.

"Baseball people, and that includes myself, are slow to change and accept new ideas,"[5] Rickey was once quoted as saying. Reviewing his career, it seems odd that he would include himself in that statement. Convinced that segregation in major league baseball was holding back the sport and society, Rickey advanced a new idea and the change it implied with tenacity, intelligence, and courage. ■

Rickey enjoys a Brooklyn Dodgers spring training game with his young grandson in 1948.

Notes

SATCHEL PAIGE

1. Leroy (Satchel) Paige, *Maybe I'll Pitch Forever*, with David Lipman, expanded ed. (Lincoln: Univ. of Neb. Pr., 1993) 227.
2. Paige 14.
3. Paige 25.
4. Paige 30.
5. Qtd. in Benjamin G. Rader, *Baseball: A History of America's Game*, 2nd ed. (Urbana: Univ. of Ill. Pr., 2002) 161-162.
6. Paige 192.
7. Qtd. in Mark Ribowsky, *Don't Look Back: Satchel Paige in the Shadows of Baseball* (New York: Simon & Schuster, 1994) 246.
8. Qtd. in David H. Nathan, *Baseball Quotations* (Jefferson, N.C.: McFarland, 1991) 158.

JACKIE ROBINSON

Chapter 1

1. Arnold Rampersad, *Jackie Robinson: A Biography* (New York: Knopf, 1997) 23.

Chapter 2

1. Qtd. in Joseph Wallace, *The Autobiography of Baseball* (New York: Abrams, 1998) 190.

Chapter 3

1. Qtd. in James A. Riley, *The Biographical Encyclopedia of the Negro Baseball Leagues* (New York: Carroll & Graf Publishers, 1994) 292.

2. Qtd. in William Brashler, *The Story of Negro League Baseball* (New York: Ticknor & Fields, 1994) 118-119.
3. Jackie Robinson, *I Never Had It Made*, with Alfred Duckett (New York: Putnam, 1972) 35.
4. Qtd. in Brashler 128.

Chapter 4

1. Murray Polner, *Branch Rickey: A Biography* (New York: Atheneum, 1982) 33-35.
2. Qtd. in Jules Tygiel, *Baseball's Great Experiment: Jackie Robinson and His Legacy*. Rev. ed. (New York: Oxford, 1997) 43.
3. J. Robinson 44-46.
4. Sharon Robinson, *Promises to Keep: How Jackie Robinson Changed America* (New York: Scholastic, 2004) 28.
5. "Rookie of the Year," *Time* 22 Sept. 1947: 72.

Chapter 5

1. J. Robinson 69.
2. J. G. Taylor Spink, "Rookie of the Year," *Sporting News* 17 Sept. 1947. <http://www.sportingnews.com/archives/jackie/art4.html>
3. *Time* 22 Sept. 1947: 70-76.

Chapter 7

1. J. Robinson 147, 149.
2. Executive Order no. 9981. "Establishing the President's Committee on Equality of Treatment and Opportunity in the Armed Services," 26 July 1948. Facsimile copy, Truman Presidential Museum and Library. <http://www.truman library.org/9981.htm>

3. Jackie Robinson and Alfred Duckett, *Breakthrough to the Big Leagues: The Story of Jackie Robinson* (New York: Harper & Row, 1965) 172.

Chapter 8
1. J. Robinson 188.
2. Qtd. in J. Robinson 284-285.
3. J. Robinson 285.
4. Qtd. in Rampersad 459.
5. Qtd. in Jules Tygiel, ed., *The Jackie Robinson Reader* (New York: Dutton, 1977) 277.
6. S. Robinson 57.
7. S. Robinson 57.

BRANCH RICKEY
1. Murray Polner, *Branch Rickey* (New York: Athenaeum, 1982) 22.
2. Polner 33-35.
3. Jackie Robinson, *I Never Had It Made,* with Alfred Duckett (New York: Putnam, 1972) 46.
4. Branch Rickey, *The American Diamond* (New York: Simon & Schuster, 1965) 45.
5. Branch Rickey, "Goodbye to Some Old Baseball Ideas," *Life* 2 Aug. 1954: 89.

Recommended Reading

BOOKS

Allen, Maury. *Jackie Robinson: A Life Remembered*. New York: Watts, 1987.

Clark, Dick, and Larry Lester, eds. *The Negro Leagues Book*. Cleveland: Soc. for Am. Baseball Research, 1994.

Falkner, David. *Great Time Coming: The Life of Jackie Robinson from Baseball to Birmingham*. New York: Simon & Schuster, 1996.

Fox, William Price. *Satchel Paige's America*. Tuscaloosa: Univ. of Ala. Pr., 2005.

Frommer, Harvey. *Rickey and Robinson: The Men Who Broke Baseball's Color Barrier*. New York: Macmillan, 1982.

Holway, John. *Josh and Satch: The Life and Times of Josh Gibson and Satchel Paige*. Westport, CT: Meckler, 1991.

Mann, Arthur. *Branch Rickey: American in Action*. Boston: Houghton, 1957.

Paige, Leroy (Satchel). *Maybe I'll Pitch Forever: A Great Baseball Player Tells the Hilarious Story Behind the Legend*. With David Lipman. Exp. ed. Lincoln: Univ. of Neb. Pr., 1993.

Polner, Murray. *Branch Rickey: A Biography*. New York: Atheneum, 1982.

Rampersad, Arnold. *Jackie Robinson: A Biography*. New York: Knopf, 1997.

Ribowsky, Mark. *A Complete History of the Negro Leagues, 1884-1955*. Rev. ed. Citadel, 2002.

—. *Don't Look Back: Satchel Paige in the Shadows of Baseball*. New York: Simon & Schuster, 1994.

Robinson, Jackie. *I Never Had It Made*. With Alfred Duckett. New York: Putnam, 1972.

Robinson, Rachel. *Jackie Robinson: An Intimate Portrait*. With Lee Daniels. New York: Abrams, 1996.

Robinson, Sharon. *Promises to Keep: How Jackie Robinson Changed America*. New York: Scholastic, 2004.

Tygiel, Jules. *Baseball's Great Experiment: Jackie Robinson and His Legacy*. Rev. ed. New York: Oxford, 1997.

WEB SITES

"Jackie Robinson and Other Baseball Highlights, 1860s-1960s." 1997. Washington, D.C.: Manuscript Division, Library of Congress; Prints and Photographs Division, Library of Congress, *American Memory*. Searches in the *American Memory* Web site bring up additional documents and photographs. <http://lcweb2.loc.gov/ammem/collections/robinson>

The Jackie Robinson Foundation. <http://jackierobinson.org>

MLB.com. 2001-2006. MLB Advanced Media, LP. Official Major League Baseball Web site, includes articles and historical player statistics. <http://mlb.mlb.com/NASApp/mlb/index.jsp>

National Baseball Hall of Fame and Museum. Searches on Paige, Robinson, and Rickey yield Hall of Fame biographies, pictures, and the text of various primary sources. <http://www.baseballhalloffame.org>

"Scrapbooks: Jackie Robinson." 2002. *SportingNews.com*. <http://www.sportingnews.com/archives/jackie/index.html>

Glossary

batting average the percentage of times that a player gets a base hit. The number of hits divided by the number of official times that the player has been at bat.

batting cage a screen placed behind the batter to stop baseballs during batting practice.

boycott to join together against, or have nothing to do with, a business in order to punish it or force it to do something.

civil rights the rights of a citizen, especially those guaranteed to all citizens of the United States, regardless of race, color, or sex, by the Bill of Rights, the 13th, 14th, 15th, 19th, 24th, and 26th amendments to the United States Constitution, and certain acts of Congress.

color barrier an unwritten rule in major league baseball that prevented blacks and whites from playing on the same teams from the late 1800's to 1947.

court-martial a military court that tries members of the armed forces who are accused of committing certain crimes.

desegregation *(dee SEHG ruh GAY shuhn)* doing away with the practice of providing separate schools and other public facilities for racial groups, especially blacks and whites.

double-header two baseball games between the same teams played on the same day.

double-play putting out two baseball players in one play.

draft the selection of persons for a special purpose, such as service in the army.

earned run a run that is scored without the aid of an error.

farm system system in which the talents of young ballplayers are cultivated and refined on minor league teams before the players move up to the major leagues.

integration *(IHN tuh GRAY shuhn)* the inclusion of people of all races on an equal basis in neighborhoods, schools, and other places.

orator *(AWR uh tuhr)* a person who can speak well in public, often with great eloquence.

pennant championship title in professional sports.

racism the belief that a particular race, especially one's own, is superior to other races.

reformatory *(rih FAWR muh TAWR ee)* an institution that seeks to help improve the behavior of young people who have broken the law.

rookie a new player on an athletic team.

satchel a small bag, especially one for carrying clothes or books.

scout a person sent out to get information about athletes or athletic teams.

segregation *(SEHG ruh GAY shuhn)* the separation of one racial group from another or from the rest of society, especially in schools, restaurants, and other public places.

sharecropper a person who farms land for the owner in return for part of the crops.

shortstop infield position in baseball between 2nd and 3rd base.

sports letter the initial of a school or other institution given as an award or trophy to members of a team.

spring training the time during which baseball players practice in a warm climate, after the winter break and before the regular playing season.

World Series the championship series of major league baseball.

Index

Page numbers in *italic* type refer to pictures.